graphics *for* URBAN DESIGN

Authors:

Bally Meeda
Neil Parkyn
David Stuart Walton

Contributors:

Andrew Bayne
Caroline Brown
Eric Holding
Matt Lally
Michael Doyle
Rob Cowan

Published by Thomas Telford Publishing, Thomas Telford Ltd, 1 Heron Quay, London E14 4JD. URL: www.thomastelford.com

Distributors for Thomas Telford books are
USA: ASCE Press, 1801 Alexander Bell Drive, Reston, VA 20191-4400, USA
Japan: Maruzen Co. Ltd, Book Department, 3–10 Nihonbashi 2-chome, Chuo-ku, Tokyo 103
Australia: DA Books and Journals, 648 Whitehorse Road, Mitcham 3132, Victoria

First published 2007
Reprinted June 2007

A catalogue record for this book is available from the British Library

Also available from Thomas Telford Books:
Urban design guidance. ISBN: 07277 3135 1
The value of urban design. ISBN: 07277 2981 0
By design: Better places to live. ISBN: 07277 3037 1
By design: Better places to work. ISBN: 07277 3398 2

ISBN: 978 0 7277 3399 3

© Thomas Telford Limited 2006

Designed and typeset by Urban Graphics
www.urban-graphics.co.uk

Printed and bound in Great Britain by Latimer Trend and Company Limited, Plymouth

David Stuart Walton 1938–2006

This book is dedicated to David Stuart Walton, planner and urban designer, who played an important part in the origination and structure of this book, but sadly passed away before it was completed.

His clarity of approach to urban design is represented in many of the images included in this book. His wit and intellect, and his ability to identify and focus on what was important, were an inspiration to those who worked with him.

The sponsors

We would like to thank the sponsors of this book for providing support, guidance and many of the examples of work within it.

Urban Graphics is a collective of creative designers and cartographers specialising in graphic design and illustration for urban design, planning and transport. They have worked throughout the UK with a variety of clients from both the public and private sectors. Effective communication is their main aim, achieved through a graphic language developed from traditional cartography and urban design techniques.

www.urban-graphics.co.uk

CABE the Commission for Architecture and the Built Environment is the Government's advisor on architecture, urban design and public space. As a public body, it encourages policymakers to create places that work for people. It helps local planning authorities apply national design policy and offers expert advice to developers and architects. It shows public sector clients how to commission buildings that meet the needs of their users. It aims to inspire the public to demand more from their buildings and spaces. Advising, influencing and inspiring, it works to create well-designed, welcoming places.

www.cabe.org.uk

Urban Design Group was founded in 1978. The Urban Design Group is a campaigning group supported by its membership – urban designers, architects, planners, engineers, surveyors, landscape architects, journalists, public artists and many more. The Urban Design Group's quarterly magazine is the leading journal in its field.

www.udg.org.uk

David Lock Associates is one of the leading town planning and urban design practices in the UK. DLA has a sixty-strong multi-disciplinary team embracing architecture, landscape and graphic design, as well as the core disciplines of planning and urban design. It offers a complete package of consultancy services to achieve creative solutions on a diversity of projects from town centre regeneration to new settlements and strategic planning to implementation.

www.davidlock.com

Gillespies specialises in creating places and spaces of quality. The practice has evolved from providing landscape design in the early 1960s to delivering comprehensive integrated services in urban design, landscape design, environmental planning and, in some regions, architecture. The firm's approach to design stems from an understanding and an appreciation of place. In a world where space is precious, it's ethos is to work with the defining characteristics and inherent qualities of place to create powerful and original ideas, which inspire clients, the stakeholders and the community – helping to create vibrant spaces that invigorate the surroundings and engage users.

www.gillespies.co.uk

John Thompson & Partners are urban designers, architects and community planning specialists with substantial experience of large-scale residential and mixed-use development in both the public and private sectors. They are involved in a wide range of projects throughout the UK and across Europe including new settlements, urban extensions, waterside developments, inner city and rural renaissance and heritage-led regeneration. The practice places a particular emphasis on delivering creative solutions to development which simultaneously achieve physical, social and environmental change.

www.jtp.co.uk

Roger Evans Associates Ltd (REAL) are architects and urban designers. Over the last decade REAL has worked on over 100 masterplans for town centres, city quarters and urban extensions across the UK and abroad. National awards include RTPI 'Planning for New Neighbourhoods', RIBA/RTPI Housing Design Awards, Civic Trust for public realm design and co-recipient of CABE Building for Life Gold Standard Awards.

ROGER EVANS ASSOCIATES

www.rogerevans.com

Foreword

Graphic design has been around since mankind discovered that images are an essential complement to words. Urban design may seem a more recent activity, but the essential components have been practised ever since we started to build and plant.

Modern pressures for both increased development and environmental stewardship strengthen the importance of communication between the designer and the client, the manager and the managed, public agencies and the general public, and the many professions involved in achieving sustainable development.

Good communication skills can establish early mutual understanding between participants in any project. This understanding can stimulate the generation of ideas that might otherwise be missed. Accurate representation of ideas can highlight their strengths and weaknesses, and help refine the preferred solution. Honest representation of the solution can help secure the agreement, commitment and enthusiasm of all involved, and establish realistic expectations of what a project can achieve.

Graphic images can communicate what may be impossible, or at least extremely long-winded, in words. Graphic design is therefore an essential component of the urban design process.

The collaboration between graphic designers and the rest of the urban design team, has not, until now, been given the scrutiny it deserves. This book gathers together a host of examples of projects that have succeeded because the teams recognised that this collaboration is essential. It has been written by practitioners with a wealth of experience. It will I'm sure be a prompt for those already engaged in graphics for urban design, and an invaluable source book for those, students or practitioners, who are coming to it for the first time.

Steven Bee

Illustrations

The plans, diagrams and graphics
contained within this book do not
always represent real proposals.
They are used to illustrate successful
graphic techniques rather than explain
specific projects.

Scope of the book

This book provides guidance on how
to use graphic techniques to stimulate
and communicate ideas through the
urban design process. It is not a guide
to the urban design process itself, nor
is it an instruction manual. Specialised
topics such as how to draw maps,
collect data, build perspectives, operate
computer software programmes, or to
manipulate photographs, are covered
more fully in technical training courses
and other publications.

Contents

How to use this book

This book highlights messages in different ways, each graphically distinct. These features appear at appropriate places and provide specific information relating to the adjacent topic.

Watchpoints

These give simple tips, hints, checklists or guidance at the end of a topic. Watchpoints are displayed in a box:

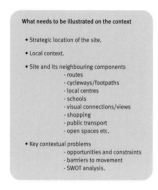

What needs to be illustrated on the context

- Strategic location of the site.
- Local context.
- Site and its neighbouring components
    - routes
    - cycleways/footpaths
    - local centres
    - schools
    - visual connections/views
    - shopping
    - public transport
    - open spaces etc.
- Key contextual problems
    - opportunities and constraints
    - barrriers to movement
    - SWOT analysis.

What it shows/ why it is good graphically

Throughout the book there are explanations of what images represent and why they succeed. This appears in bullet points under the headings shown below:

What it shows:
- range of alternative land uses within the grid format of a new quarter of Edinburgh, showing the inbuilt flexibility of the typical development block
- variety of street types and appropriate uses fronting them
- alternative uses for the core of the block, including employment, 'mews' housing and public space.

Why it is good graphically:
- shows concept without being precise
- hand-drawn to emphasis the ideas stage
- all uses annotated.

Case studies

There are four case studies that illustrate how graphics techniques have been employed on commissioned projects. They appear on coloured pages:

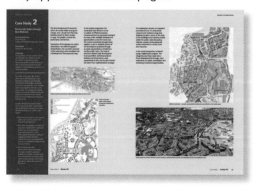

Ticks and crosses

Comparisons of good and bad examples are made and are illustrated with a tick (good example) or a a cross (bad example):

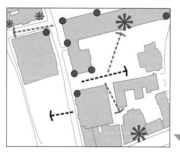

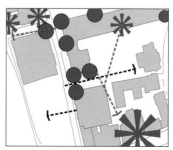

Introduction

This book provides a guide to producing
high quality plans and illustrations
for urban design projects; presenting
material that is clear, relevant,
accessible, honest and attractive.

0.1
The purpose of this book

The book is for:

- urban designers, architects, planners, landscape architects, surveyors and engineers engaged in urban design projects
- graphic designers, artists and the producers and publishers of urban design work
- those who commission graphics for urban design
- educators and students in urban design and graphics.

The graphical language of urban design has an important role to play in promoting urban quality; creating visions which inspire and motivate; engaging communities and others involved in planning and development; and presenting information objectively and honestly for assessment purposes.

2-D illustration of Nottingham city centre masterplan

3-D computer model of Spencer Dock, Dublin

3-D computer model of Fletchergate, Nottingham

Street level artists perspective, Mill Square, Peterborough

The technology now available provides designers and producers of graphic images with enormous choice. The graphic vocabulary continues to evolve. This brings exciting opportunities and challenges in choosing the right mix of techniques combining computer-generated images, hand-drawn plans and sketches and photography in new ways. This book aims to help urban design teams select the most appropriate form of graphic communication for the type of project, and the distinct stages of a project.

Until now there has been no reference work, no guide to the range of techniques that has emerged through practice. This book is intended to provide such a guide, but it is not the last word. Techniques will continue to evolve through practice. We hope this guide will be widely used and help those involved to develop better graphic techniques in urban design, furthering the communication of ideas.

There are people and organisations who do the stuff of this book very well. They have provided the body of work from which we have drawn to illustrate this book, and offer examples of good practice for us all to follow.

3-D computer block model of South Bank, Peterborough

0.2
Effective communication

Realising successful urban projects depends upon effective communication.

The Government's modernised planning regime places strong emphasis on the full involvement of local communities at every stage of policy and project development. This requires first-rate communication throughout the consultation process.

The teams involved in the design and delivery of urban design projects include a wide range of professions and specialists who need to communicate effectively and speedily with each other. Projects can be compromised or even fail through breakdowns in communication that lead to misunderstanding.

There are two sides to the communication process. Information and vision need to be transmitted to the target audience using the right media and techniques. In their turn, the audience must be able to understand and engage with the message. Visual techniques play an important role in transferring knowledge and creating a basis for debate.

Public consultation for East Cowes masterplan

The array of techniques and media can be overwhelming, but irrespective of how well these techniques have been mastered, selecting the right form of presentation for the particular audience at the particular stage in the urban design process is the key to success.

Throughout the development process, from the initial concepts to the detailed proposals, the effective communication of information and ideas depends on several interrelated factors including:

- type of information to be presented
- clarity of information
- accuracy and validity of information
- audience awareness and levels of understanding
- media selected to present information.

0.3
Teamwork and leadership

No guidance can substitute for a well-led, talented and committed design team.

The project designers (architects, urban designers, landscape architects etc.) must be able to recognise when the job switches to the illustrative designers – the graphic designers and artists. There is no definitive point at which this should happen; it depends on the skills in the team, the stage of the project and the messages to be conveyed. Equally, the graphic designers need freedom to exercise their skills and imagination but not to the extent that the graphics, however attractive, detract from the essential urban design messages.

As the range of urban design products grow, so do the range of specialists involved: perspective artists, computer-aided design (CAD) designers, photographic and photo-editing specialists, cartographers, GIS operatives, artists, even cartoonists, may need to be called upon to support the core professionals and graphic designers on the team.

Strong leadership, understanding and deploying the right skills at the right time, listening to all, then deciding is generally the best way forward.

Interactive computer presentation at Bathgate public consultation

Guiding principles for graphics in urban design

chapter 1

1.1 Choice of techniques │ 1.2 Honesty and integrity │ 1.3 House style │
1.4 Clarity │ 1.5 Hand-drawn and computer graphics

The principles set out in this chapter should apply irrespective of the stage of the design process. They are based on convention rather than statute, but will help all those involved to make consistent and appropriate graphics choices, ensuring not only attractive visuals but also effective communication of information.

1.1
Choice of techniques

Graphics for urban design projects fall within four basic techniques. Deciding which to use in any given situation needs careful consideration of three things:

- type of information (the message)
- media (the means of communicating the message)
- style (the look and character of the message).

Graphic style attracts the viewer, who can then engage with well-edited and structured information.

Presentations (publications/exhibitions/screen shows) should be coherent narratives built out of a series of visual images that describe the project vision. Presentations and visual techniques can be considered effective only if a clear message is conveyed and the intended audience accurately informed. This depends on the clarity and appropriateness of the message and how well this has been tailored to its specific audience.

Information is presented in or derived from one of four techniques:

- conceptual
- analytical
- measurable
- perceptual.

1.1.1 Conceptual techniques

These are used to encapsulate and convey a particularly important or strong idea. At its simplest it may be a cartoon, an ideogram or a visual sound bite. More complex means include painted artworks or mood boards, which convey atmosphere or precedent without committing to form.

Such techniques can present provisional and unresolved ideas in a way that encourages the audience to engage in their further development. They should aid thinking about the built environment in terms of concepts and aspirations rather than the familiar, concrete images which some participants may be more comfortable.

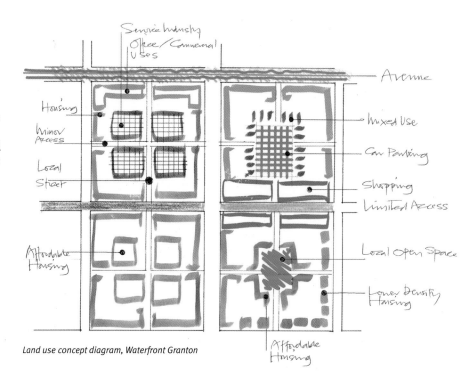

Land use concept diagram, Waterfront Granton

What it shows:

- range of alternative land uses within the grid format of a new quarter of Edinburgh, showing the inbuilt flexibility of the typical development block
- variety of street types and appropriate uses fronting them
- alternative uses for the core of the block, including employment, 'mews' housing and public space.

Why it is good graphically:

- shows the concept without being overly precise
- hand-drawn to emphasise the ideas stage
- informal annotation style appropriate.

1.1.2 Analytical techniques

Graphic representation can help identify the nature of problems and possible solutions. Techniques can display patterns of behaviour and activity that are influenced by spatial layout. The image illustrated here shows how complex patterns of activity are more easily discerned when portrayed graphically rather than in data or text. The implications of such patterns for urban design can be communicated in a logical and understandable manner.

Flow levels

High

Low

Pedestrian flows in central Boston

What it shows:

- patterns of spatial accessibility in central Boston: knowing these patterns helps us to understand and estimate how pedestrians use the area
- a probable hierarchy of pedestrian intensification: further analysis (land use, figure ground and connectivity) would tell us why the intensification is where it is and why some areas expected to be intense are not.

Why it is good graphically:

- displays high intensity values in the hottest colour (red) and low intensity values in the coldest colour (blue)
- neutral base-map allows the analytical information to stand out
- all extraneous map data has been removed, leaving only the necessary detail to orientate the viewer
- the key clearly indicates the levels of pedestrian flow.

1.1.3 Measurable techniques

Measurable information is usually presented in two-dimensional form and allows precise data to be conveyed. It provides an accurate baseline from which detailed design of discrete components can be reliably co-ordinated.

Computer-aided design (CAD) plan showing residential layout, Ravensbourne

What it shows:

- precise relationships between elements shown in plan
- CAD drawing format allows precise calculations of dimensions and areas, equally applicable to site plans and building layouts
- provides a reference framework for more detailed information and the basis for three-dimensional form – also used to present site and building data and to define key relationships.

Why it is good graphically:

- variety of line weights to emphasise different elements
- simple graphic style
- can be fully dimensioned.

1.1.4 Perceptual techniques

Perceptual techniques help a general audience understand how proposed designs might look and feel. They are generally based upon forms of perspective that closely represent the way the built environment is seen and can have varying degrees of realism. All hinge upon the fixed nature of the view, which makes the viewpoint important. Eye-level views give the observer the sense of being in a space, while aerial perspectives can bring masterplans to life and make it easier for people to orientate themselves within the proposals. These techniques are often useful in visioning processes because they present an exciting, coherent image without having to resolve more detailed issues. However, caution should be exercised in using aerial perspectives alone, for instance, as these are views very few are likely to experience in reality.

3-D computer model, Nottingham

Hand-drawn aerial perspective, Tally Ho

What it shows:

- indicative proposal for a clustered residential development in context showing character, scale and interrelationships of buildings
- demonstrates the intended variety of built form and external spaces
- emphasises the contrast between the cluster of development and the broad open landscape beyond
- conveys the intended character and quality of the development rather than actual architectural detail.

Why it is good graphically:

- hand-drawn image emphasises provisional stage of design
- user-friendly and accessible
- limited but appropriate colour palette
- colours used to identify different elements clearly.

What it shows:

- indicates the form, scale and character of a proposed central covered street within a new city-centre complex, showing it as a varied and lively route
- indicates how the street in section is made vibrant by several levels of shopping and leisure uses with views and links between them
- emphasises how the space, although weather-protected, is animated by natural light and landscaping.

Why it is good graphically:

- cropped perspective emphasises the particular character of part of the proposed development
- use of planting and people conveys a sense of scale and the level of activity expected in the completed development
- emphasises the importance of architectural detail to the quality and character of the development.

1.2
Honesty and integrity

Illustration and graphics are a powerful means of communication. This raises the issue of responsibility for those who commission and those who produce urban design images.

Graphic presentations are used not only to communicate, but also to persuade and convince. In trying to present the potential of a project, however, it is possible to produce seductive images that could be misleading or may be misinterpreted. 'Artistic licence' may go beyond the need to present a positive message and promote the project. Attractive illustrations of proposed places can prove less than honest in projecting the eventual outcome.

Watchpoints

- Ensure all involved understand the purpose of the illustration.
- Clearly communicate the level of precision or impression to the audience.
- Use the appropriate technique to convey information – analytical, conceptual, perceptual or measurable.
- Understand the strengths and limitations of hand-drawn and computer-generated techniques before deciding which to use.
- Avoid using graphics to mislead the audience.

1.3
House style

Graphical representation allows the expression of a distinct personality and house style in the graphics associated with a particular organisation or project. This may be expressed through the designer's choice of typeface, colour palette, layout templates and treatment of graphic figures, possibly reinforced by a project or corporate logo. These in turn promote:

- consistency
- brand
- visual identity
- quality
- authority.

Visual consistency is particularly valuable when presenting diverse urban design projects to varied audiences, over time and at different stages of project development. A strong graphic identity conveys energy and consistency.

House-styles and templates can make production more efficient, avoiding the need to start from scratch with each image or document.

Watchpoints

- Make corporate or house style guidelines available.
- Pre-install necessary templates before starting project.
- One-off or bespoke projects may not necessarily follow a corporate style.

Scunthorpe Urban Renaissance

1.4
Clarity

The most effective illustrations for urban design projects are those that have been subjected to critical editing of the source material and careful design of the figure. The example opposite has been carefully edited from the original sketch and base map to show only the relevant information keeping it clear and legible.

Origination should take into account the possibility of a drawing being copied or reproduced. The processes involved can diminish or degrade the quality of the original line work.

Watchpoints

- Convey the key information directly without background distraction.
- Use colour, tone and line logically to express relative intensity or importance.
- Make a limited number of points effectively.
- Consistent bases allow easy cross-reference within sets of illustrations.
- Suppress irrelevant detail.
- Bear in mind future use or adaptation of images.

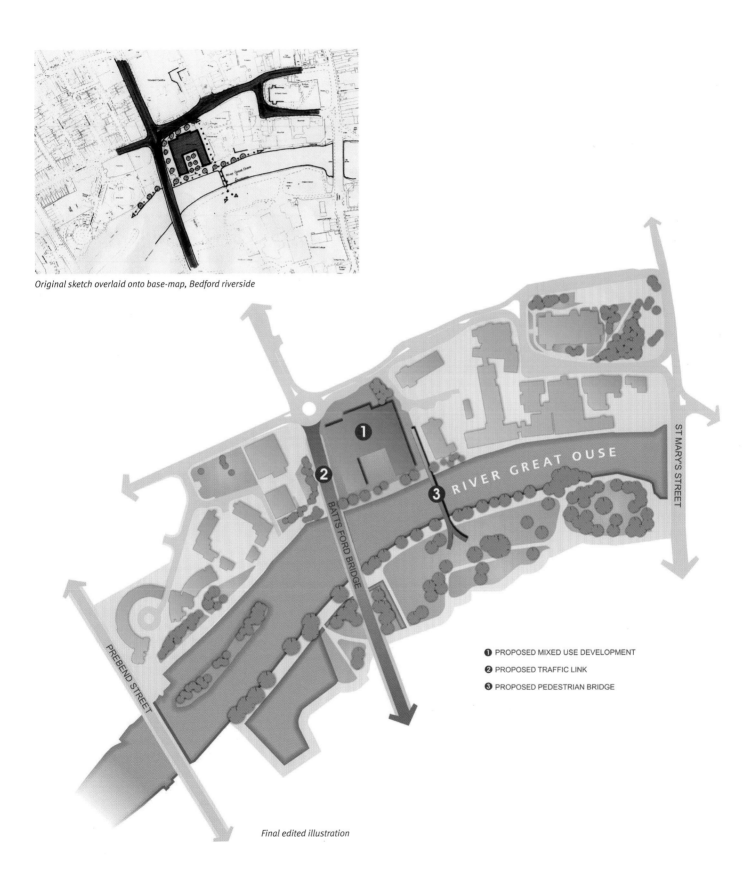

Original sketch overlaid onto base-map, Bedford riverside

RIVER GREAT OUSE

ST MARY'S STREET

BATTS FORD BRIDGE

PREBEND STREET

❶ PROPOSED MIXED USE DEVELOPMENT

❷ PROPOSED TRAFFIC LINK

❸ PROPOSED PEDESTRIAN BRIDGE

Final edited illustration

Computer-generated image using 3-D modelling software, Nottingham

1.5
Hand-drawn and computer graphics

Most of the methods of graphical communication shown in this book can be created by traditional hand-drawn methods or computer graphics.

Computer-generated graphics are generally turned to when either a level of accuracy is required that cannot be achieved by hand, or when complex tools are needed to speed the design process.

Selecting the most appropriate medium is not always straightforward. Whether hand-drawn, computer-generated or a combination of both, first identify the purpose and desired character of the image to be created. The technique or technology should not be allowed to dominate the message to be conveyed.

Hand-drawn sketch using pencil crayon and ink, Urban Realm Strategy, Aberdeen

Hand-drawn images make use of traditional media such as pencil, crayon, felt pen, marker pen, ink and watercolour. These mediums can convey a lively impression without being too definitive. They are easily shared by a group, involving all in developing ideas. They are familiar to non-professionals, encouraging their participation. They can be used anywhere.

Computer graphics provide an enormous range of communication techniques and devices. Data can be converted to image very quickly. Ideas can be easily saved, duplicated, transmitted and displayed.

With the increasing availability and utility of computers and design software, the immediacy and uniqueness of the bespoke hand-drawn image is once again a symbol of quality and distinctiveness.

Organisations and individuals develop their own preferences and abilities. While it is always good to explore new ways of communicating, it is best to be comfortable with any technique before using it in public. Don't be driven by fashion or dazzled by technology. Choose the medium most appropriate to the audience.

*Hand-drawn plan using technical drawing pens,
felt pens and pencil crayon, Newport*

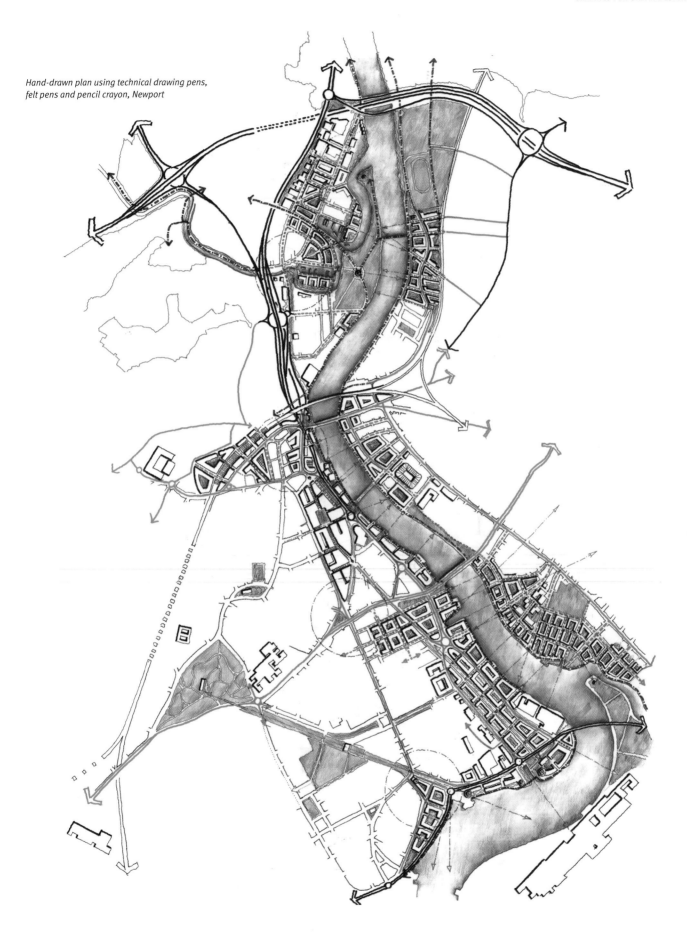

Hand-drawn images

Effective in:

- Quickly communicating simple ideas.

- Emphasising the provisional status of proposals.

- Creating a unique personality.

- Explaining concepts without being over-precise.

- Conveying the atmosphere and vibrancy of a place.

- Encouraging participation – tools and materials are inexpensive, easily transported and useable by all.

Weaknesses:

- May not be accurate.

- Not easy to update drawings in series.

- Changing views or designs generally means redrawing.

- Can lack clarity.

Computer graphics

Effective in:

- Accurately mapping information.

- Presenting definitive solutions.

- Simulating complex views.

- Making changes easily.

- Conveniently storing and retrieving many complex images.

- Linking to external information or databases.

- Replicating and transmitting information to others.

Weaknesses:

- Can be expensive to set up.

- Difficult to share access.

- Have a finished/resolved visual feel.

- Extensive training may be required.

- Systems failures can be difficult to handle.

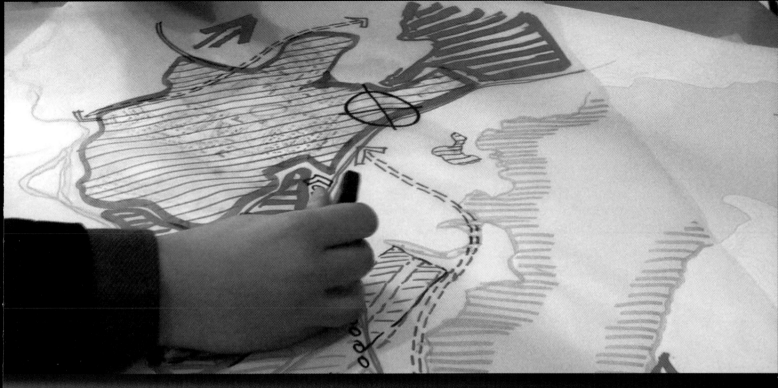

Graphics in the urban design process

This chapter explains the ways in
which graphical representation
can aid communication in each of
the main stages of the urban

2.1
Contextual analysis

A shared understanding of the context of a scheme is the foundation of a successful project. Aspects of the breadth and diversity of the context of a scheme can be helpfully communicated graphically. Images can convey:

- the overall urban/rural structure
- discrete areas: uses, amenities, routes, open spaces and landscape
- opportunities and constraints arising from the setting and how they might be addressed
- special features of the area to be addressed.

Different contextual issues may often need to be illustrated at different scales and in different ways. From regional to local context, maps, plans, diagrams and photos will present different levels of information. Where images at widely differing scales are used, graphic devices to link them, such as inset maps or blow-ups, help orientate the audience and speed understanding.

2.1.1 Setting

Understanding the implications of the setting of a site on its development potential is an essential early component of the urban design process. The main or special features of a site and its location can be encapsulated in a diagram. These will include geographic features but also features of historic significance, views, connections with other places and elements of local distinctiveness.

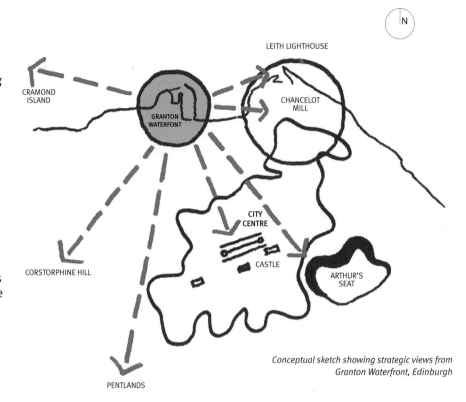

Conceptual sketch showing strategic views from Granton Waterfront, Edinburgh

What it shows:

- presents the direct relationship between the major regeneration opportunity of Edinburgh's Granton Waterfront to the city centre
- indicates how the Granton site benefits from long views to important landmarks
- emphasises the close and direct relationship of Granton to the historic core of the city
- suggests that the framework of views and its strategic location are both distinct assets of the new urban quarter.

Why it is good graphically:

- hand-drawn sketch emphasises conceptual overview rather than measurable information
- views highlighted in blue
- site highlighted in a tint of red.

2.1.2 Locating the site

A sequence of maps at successively larger scales helps guide the user through increasing levels of detail from the strategic to the local to the site-specific. At each level the graphics should be appropriate to the detail required at that scale.

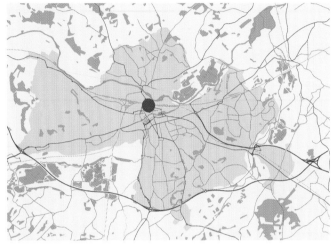

Greater Reading

Strategic context
Shows the strategic location of the site related to:

- transport links
- pattern of urban development
- geographical features.

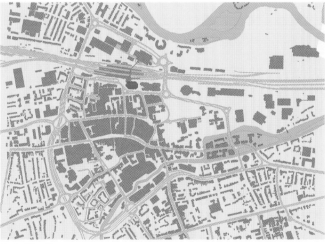

Central Reading

Local context
Shows how the site is located in relation to:

- transport links and local hierarchy of routes
- urban density and scale
- general features including rivers and main green spaces.

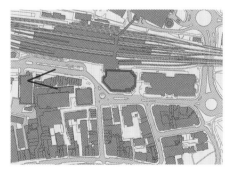

Reading railway station

Site context
Shows the precise site boundary in relation to:

- roads
- footpaths
- buildings
- plot boundaries.

Satellite, aerial or terrestrial photography can help at all scales. If terrestrial, indicating the camera location is important.

2.1.3 Contextual appraisal

Understanding the physical form of the immediate surroundings of a site, and the history that has shaped it, helps the design team create new development that reinforces local character and distinctiveness. It also identifies existing elements that compromise such character and might offer opportunities for adaptation or replacement.

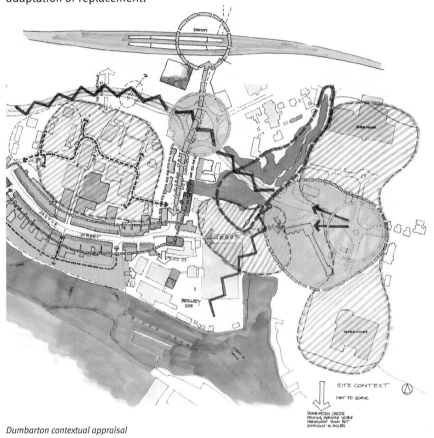

Dumbarton contextual appraisal

What needs to be illustrated on context plans:

- Enough of the surrounding area to locate the study area/site.

- Site and its neighbouring features:
  - roads/railways/waterways
  - cycleways/footpaths
  - local centres
  - schools
  - visual connections/views
  - shopping
  - public transport
  - open spaces etc.

- Known contextual issues:
  - opportunities and constraints
  - barriers to movement
  - SWOT analysis (strengths, weaknesses, opportunities and threats).

▭▭⇥	Main connections
▭	Areas with strong frontages
●	Areas of opportunity
▨	Poorly defined areas
∿∿	Barriers to movement and links
○	Existing or potential nodes
◗	Riverside area of development potential
◄	Trees and vegetation
→	Key views
⋯⋯	Pedestrian routes
▬	Important buildings

What it shows:

- a general summary of the urban character of a town centre, describing its existing structure and regeneration opportunities

- the very close relationship between the town centre and the riverfront which could be reinforced by appropriate development

- the context and hinterland for riverfront regeneration, including key routes and links, important buildings and views.

Why it is good graphically:

- all elements shown by distinct colour coding, symbols or patterns

- hand-drawn diagram emphasising the early, provisional stage of the project

- minimal annotation avoiding clutter

- 'not to scale' discourages assumptions of inappropriate accuracy

- logical colours used, e.g. water bodies blue, vegetation green.

2.2
Spatial analysis

The presentation of the parameters of a project for analysis can take many forms:

- plans and diagrammatic plans
- graphical techniques for presenting data and statistical information – graphs, bar charts, pie-charts etc.
- conceptual diagrams illustrating ways of thinking and planning.

The following are almost invariably required:

- opportunities and constraints plan
- development area/form analysis
- landscape/open space analysis
- movement plan.

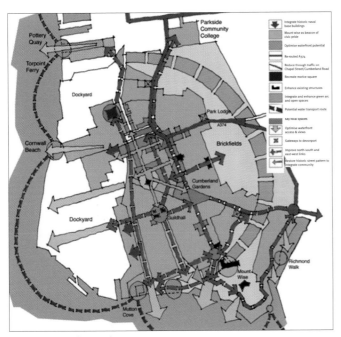

Opportunities and constraints

Development area

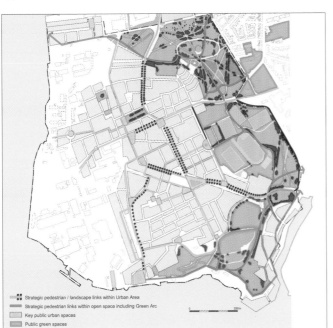

Open space analysis

Movement

2.2.1 Figure ground

This is a graphical device for identifying and differentiating the built-up areas from the public realm and open space to emphasise development patterns, density and scale. Buildings are in solid colour to contrast with spaces. It is created from a map-base but shows only the solids (built form) and voids (open spaces and public realm).

Stevenage

Oxford

Banbury

Stratford-upon-Avon

What it shows:

- solid (built form) and void (open space) to indicate urban grain
- different patterns of built form/typology
- intensity of development
- main routes and corridors.

Why it is good graphically:

- strong contrast between buildings and spaces
- all extraneous detail removed.

2.2.2 Nolli plan

This differentiates between public and private spaces, showing public areas as white, including areas within buildings such as churches or courtyards, and privately owned buildings and land parcels in a solid colour.

Hungate, York
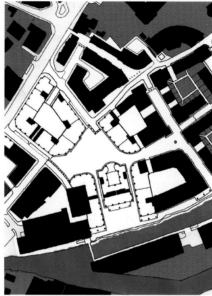

What it shows:

- publicly accessible areas
- space within blocks
- entry points to public space.

Why it is good graphically:

- strong contrast between the public (white) and private (grey) spaces
- all extraneous detail removed.

2.2.3 Character areas

This plan identifies areas of discrete and distinct character within a wider urban or rural area. It focuses attention on areas of particular interest and may be used to emphasise historic development patterns. It can be presented on a map base or a figure ground; as keyed categories or by annotation onto each area. The emphasis is on broad characterisation of urban grain. Character areas may include transitional and buffer zones.

Swindon

Town Centre/Core
The "Railway Village"
Nineteenth Century Inner Suburbs
Mid Twentieth Century Commercial Redevelopment

What it shows:

- areas and extent of distinct character
- differences in urban grain
- interfaces between areas.

Why it is good graphically:

- areas coloured differently for easy identification
- all extraneous detail removed.

2.2.4 Landmarks and monuments

Presenting these on a plan not only illustrates and emphasises areas/points of great importance or sensitivity, but also helps orientate those familiar with the area. Signs or symbols on a base-map, exaggerated in scale clearly indicate the location (as some monuments may not be visible on a map) and the hierarchy of significance.

Chancery Lane, London

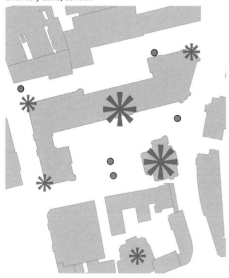

✳ Major Landmark

✳ Minor Landmark

● Monument

What it shows:

- location of landmark buildings, features or significant monuments
- relative importance of landmarks
- relationships between landmarks.

Why it is good graphically:

- landmarks emphasised with a star in bold colour
- monuments highlighted in red (the colour of importance or sensitivity).

2.2.5 Designated areas

Plans indicate areas of protection, preservation, management, or restoration of historic importance, natural or scientific interest, or resources such as forests, soils and water. They are normally presented on a base-map with definitive boundary lines. The differentiation of designated areas is illustrated by use of tone, texture or pattern within the boundary.

Nottingham

☐ Conservation Area
||||||| Historic Park

What it shows:

- boundaries of conservation areas
- special zones within
- relative proportion of designated areas.

Why it is good graphically:

- boundary emphasised as a definitive line
- conservation areas coloured to make clear which side of the line is designated (this may not be clear if extracts from the map are used separately)
- historic park delineated with a pattern
- consistent use of colour.

2.2.6 Views

Plans highlight lines of visibility, view corridors and panorama vantage points. Some views may be protected. It is normally presented on a map base or figure ground.

Nottingham

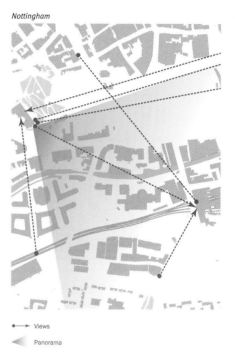

●──▸ Views

◂ Panorama

What it shows:

- key views
- key panoramas.

Why it is good graphically:

- shows viewpoint, direction and viewed object
- consistent line weight, type (i.e. dash) and colour
- graphics indicate the extent of the panorama
- transparent colour allows the map base to show through.

2.2.7 Listed buildings

These plans identify buildings, structures and monuments that are statutorily or locally protected for their architectural or historic interest. Buildings are shown in a solid, bold colour, usually red (colours can be graded according to listing status). Such plans can be combined with conservation area plans if the amount of information is not likely to confuse the user.

Nottingham

■ Listed Buildings

What it shows:

- location of buildings and spaces
- distribution of listed buildings.

Why it is good graphically:

- listed buildings shown in solid red (the colour of importance or sensitivity)
- all extraneous detail removed.

2.2.8 Historic evolution

A sequence of maps of a place from earlier periods in its history can emphasise how a settlement or landscape has evolved over time. They can be presented as a set of individual historic Ordnance Survey© maps in their original form, but can be more easily compared if presented on a common base to a common scale. Digital storage of historic maps enables maps of different periods to be superimposed. This is particularly useful for historic landscape and urban characterisation.

Reading 1900

Reading 1995

What it shows:

- incremental changes in urban grain
- relationship of built form to open space
- changing character of specific areas
- relative intensity of development.

Why it is good graphically:

- strong contrast between buildings and spaces
- all extraneous detail removed
- sequences presented at the same scale
- easy cross-reference.

2.2.9 Pedestrian movement

This illustrates 'fundamental use patterns' in an area – where people move and where they stop. Information is presented on a single plan or a series to illustrate changes in patterns of activity over different time periods, for different categories or user, or before and after a design intervention.

Trafalgar Square

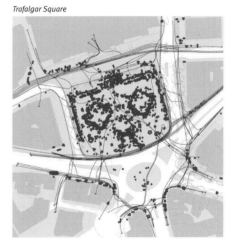

- • Stationary people
- → Moving people

What it shows:

- a snapshot of how people use the area around a square – where they move and where they stop.

Why it is good graphically:

- the difference between categories of information (stationary people vs. moving people) visually emphasised by varying both colour and form.
- forms appropriate to the activity depicted: spots easily interpreted as stasis; lines as movement
- neutral base-map allowing the observed activity to stand out, while buildings, roads and spaces are still discernable
- all extraneous detail removed.

2.2.10 Spatial accessibility analysis

Such plans illustrate the relative accessibility of different areas of a place, which exerts a powerful influence on pedestrian, cyclist and vehicular movement patterns and, by extension, on the social and economic characteristics of urban areas. The information for different modes of travel can be presented individually or as a series of maps to illustrate changes in patterns of spatial accessibility at different scales, or before and after a design intervention. Base-maps may be included for local studies but are usually omitted for broader, strategic studies.

Spatial accessibilty

High

Low
● Unlinks (points where streets or walkways cross but don't intersect)

Spatial accessibility map, Greater London

What it shows:

- a network of streets and public spaces represented as a set of the fewest and longest lines that cover all the space and make all connections

- each line is coloured according to a quantitative spatial accessibility value.

Why it is good graphically:

- displays spaces with high spatial accessibility in the hottest colour (red) and low spatial accessibility in the coolest colour (blue)

- allows easy cross-comparison between baseline conditions and design options

- all extraneous map data has been removed, leaving only the necessary detail

- key clearly indicates the range of values.

2.3
Statistical analysis

This type of analysis is normally represented by a combination of quantitative data attributed to a graphic. Charts, graphs, tables, etc. can convey quite complex data, and are particularly useful for comparing sets of information against each other.

The manipulation of such data may not seem central to the urban design process, but graphic representations can help urban design teams understand the dynamics of activity in the project area, the trends that are likely to influence the success of the proposed development, and identify and balance competing demands or pressures.

2.3.1 Charts

Two-dimensional charts can present quite complex information in an unequivocal and easily interpreted form. They are particularly useful for illustrating the relative significance of sets of variables.

Bar chart

Bar charts can be either horizontal or vertical. The length of bars may reflect the total value, or bars may present relative proportions of components.

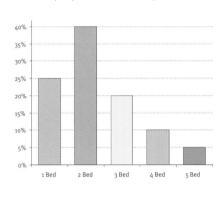

Line chart

Line charts or graphs show continuous data, for example over time, for a single variable. Variables can be combined for comparison on a single graph.

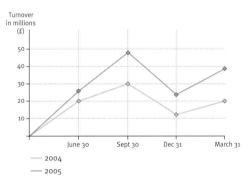

Pie chart

Pie charts are divided into sectors proportional in angle and area to the relative size of the quantities represented.

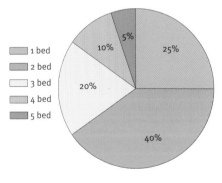

Radar chart

A radar chart, or star or spider graph, is used primarily as a means of comparison between data sets against several variables.

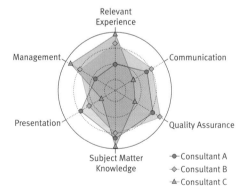

2.3.2 Map-based statistics

The maps and diagrams here demonstrate how it is possible to present quantitative data graphically, so that a clear message is visible both as a graphic and as data.

Traffic flows

The statistics presented opposite relate to peak hour traffic movements by car and public transport to six other zones. Three types of movement are shown:

- internal trips within the area
- trips to the central area
- trips to the other five zones.

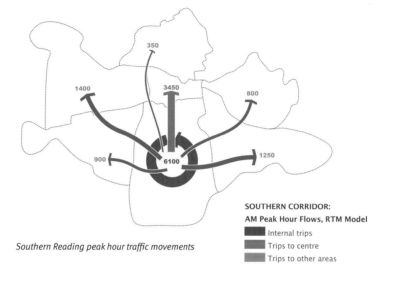

Southern Reading peak hour traffic movements

SOUTHERN CORRIDOR:
AM Peak Hour Flows, RTM Model
- Internal trips
- Trips to centre
- Trips to other areas

Unemployment split

This map uses data on unemployment by census ward. The size of the circles represents the level of unemployment within 3 kilometres of major railway stations.

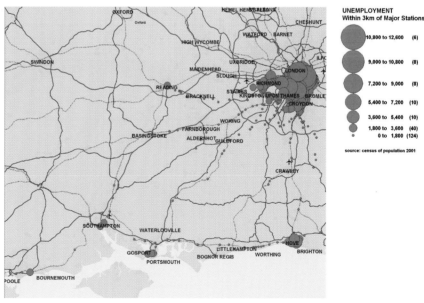

Unemployment within 3km of major stations

UNEMPLOYMENT
Within 3km of Major Stations

10,800 to 12,600	(6)
9,000 to 10,800	(8)
7,200 to 9,000	(8)
5,400 to 7,200	(10)
3,600 to 5,400	(10)
1,800 to 3,600	(40)
0 to 1,800	(124)

source: census of population 2001

Population density

This map shows population density by census ward across south-west London. The data is presented in tones that portray relative population density. High density is the darkest tone and low density the lightest. The wider base-map is in a neutral shade, helping with orientation without distracting from the data presented. Using tones within a limited colour range helps to emphasise the distribution of different densities of a single variable. The title explains the basis on which density has been calculated.

People per hectare 2001

100 +
70 - 100
45 - 70
30 - 45
15 - 30
5 - 15
0 - 5

Source: census of population, 2001

Pedestrian count

This map presents pedestrian flows surveyed within a city centre. By expressing the volume of flow along routes in the width of the lines, the overall pattern and intensity of movement is expressed graphically. The overlaid figures provide the actual numbers of pedestrians without diluting the message and the neutral base-map allows the important information to stand out.

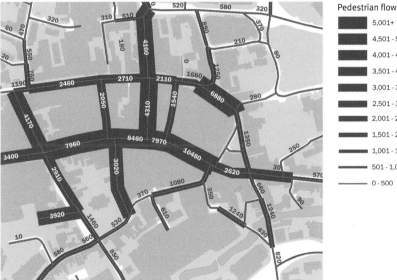

Pedestrian flow

5,001+
4,501 - 5000
4,001 - 4,500
3,501 - 4,000
3,001 - 3,500
2,501 - 3,000
2,001 - 2,500
1,501 - 2,000
1,001 - 1,500
501 - 1,000
0 - 500

2.4
Conceptual analysis

Graphic images can help order and communicate the abstract concepts that the team uses to resolve issues and analyse opportunities. Flow charts, critical path analysis, Venn diagrams and many other techniques can help, but communicating complex ideas or processes can be made easier by graphic devices.

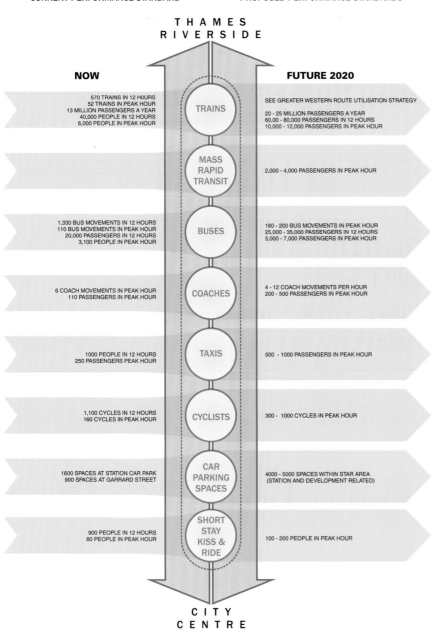

CURRENT PERFORMANCE STANDARD · PROPOSED PERFORMANCE STANDARDS

THAMES RIVERSIDE

NOW · **FUTURE 2020**

TRAINS
- 570 TRAINS IN 12 HOURS
- 52 TRAINS IN PEAK HOUR
- 13 MILLION PASSENGERS A YEAR
- 40,000 PEOPLE IN 12 HOURS
- 6,000 PEOPLE IN PEAK HOUR

- SEE GREATER WESTERN ROUTE UTILISATION STRATEGY
- 20 - 25 MILLION PASSENGERS A YEAR
- 60,00 - 80,000 PASSENGERS IN 12 HOURS
- 10,000 - 12,000 PASSENGERS IN PEAK HOUR

MASS RAPID TRANSIT
- 2,000 - 4,000 PASSENGERS IN PEAK HOUR

BUSES
- 1,330 BUS MOVEMENTS IN 12 HOURS
- 110 BUS MOVEMENTS IN PEAK HOUR
- 20,000 PASSENGERS IN 12 HOURS
- 3,100 PEOPLE IN PEAK HOUR

- 160 - 200 BUS MOVEMENTS IN PEAK HOUR
- 25,000 - 35,000 PASSENGERS IN 12 HOURS
- 5,000 - 7,000 PASSENGERS IN PEAK HOUR

COACHES
- 6 COACH MOVEMENTS IN PEAK HOUR
- 110 PASSENGERS IN PEAK HOUR

- 4 - 12 COACH MOVEMENTS PER HOUR
- 200 - 500 PASSENGERS IN PEAK HOUR

TAXIS
- 1000 PEOPLE IN 12 HOURS
- 250 PASSENGERS PEAK HOUR

- 500 - 1000 PASSENGERS IN PEAK HOUR

CYCLISTS
- 1,100 CYCLES IN 12 HOURS
- 160 CYCLES IN PEAK HOUR

- 300 - 1000 CYCLES IN PEAK HOUR

CAR PARKING SPACES
- 1600 SPACES AT STATION CAR PARK
- 900 SPACES AT GARRARD STREET

- 4000 - 5000 SPACES WITHIN STAR AREA
- (STATION AND DEVELOPMENT RELATED)

SHORT STAY KISS & RIDE
- 900 PEOPLE IN 12 HOURS
- 60 PEOPLE IN PEAK HOUR

- 100 - 200 PEOPLE IN PEAK HOUR

CITY CENTRE

The diagram describes the concept of an 'interchange spine' stretching from a city centre location to the River Thames within which different modes of transport coincide, enabling changes between modes while minimising the 'interchange penalty' – the time it takes to change between modes. The diagram indicates current and future potential movements or flows as 'performance standards'.

2.5
Public participation

Public participation is a key element in preparing most plans and projects, whether for a local development framework, an action plan for an area or a masterplan for a proposed development. The graphics tools for participation relate to the three categories or steps in the process:

i)   initial engagement

ii) workshops

iii) preliminary proposals.

Each requires a different graphic design treatment.

Graphics support for public participation has to help attract attention, stimulate interest and encourage involvement. Contextual studies should have identified the diversity of the community of interest, the level of existing knowledge of the project and the level of support or antipathy to the overall objective. All of these will influence the choice of graphical presentation.

High quality production can help establish authority and commitment to the project, but can distance the team from the community. Impromptu advertising can be eye-catching, but is not usually sufficient to stimulate wide interest. A selection of techniques with an overall identity, perhaps a project logo, gives the best chance of capturing a wide audience.

2.5.1 The initial engagement

Whatever techniques are used, the material must express issues, choice and flexibility and not, at this stage, solutions. A certain softness is required, not hard-edged precision that might imply decisions have already been made. The graphics will be for posters and flyers advertising the event, for information on the nature of the area and possibly the main choices involved.

Improvised graphics have immediacy and are eye-catching.

Using the project logo to identify team members and facilitators is a good idea – badges or T-shirts are usually sufficient. Over-elaborate efforts could appear extravagant and be counter-productive.

Publicity posters in local shops increase local awareness and emphasise local commitment.

Children expressing their thoughts and ideas through drawing, colouring and painting.

Engaging children can be relatively easy, and their unconstrained and unselfconscious involvement can stimulate new ideas. It is also a good way of engaging sometimes more reticent adults. Simple and novel graphics can help, and materials with which they are familiar will encourage them to join in.

Initial graphic style should be informal compared with the more polished products of later stages.

A co-ordinated team and well-prepared graphics emphasise commitment and promote credibility.

Sharing views, thoughts and ideas can be encouraged by a carefully designed setting.

2.5.2 Workshops

The most important participants are likely to be unfamiliar with plans and concepts of development. Facilitators and other project members must be trained to help people get used to the formats being used, and encourage them to put forward their ideas. Standardised base-maps or plans will ensure that all groups produce ideas that can be easily aggregated. Models or cards at the scale of buildings, blocks of buildings or areas of development can help people understand the basic concepts and implications of layout, density and planning.

Keep it simple, clear and relevant

Use base-maps where necessary – make sure they are clearly annotated.

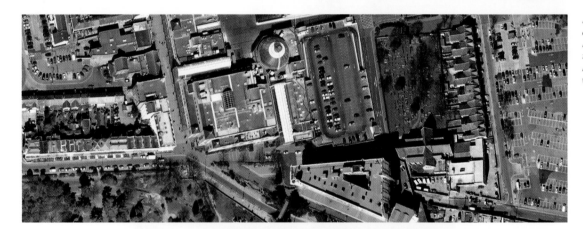

Photographs, especially aerial photographs, can help people orientate themselves, find their home, their route to work/school, etc.

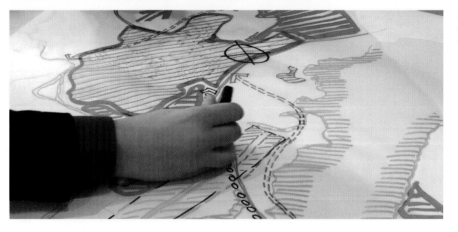

Use tracing or acetate overlays to try out early ideas.

Have trained illustrators available to help

Illustrators on hand to help transfer ideas onto paper.

Provide a variety of pens, markers and other drawing tools. Use large ones and provide plenty of bright colours. Make sure they work first!

Drawings are not the only way of communicating. The public should be invited to express their concerns in whichever medium makes them feel a part of the process.

Provide ample opportunity for feedback

Feedback forms should be designed to encourage people to complete them, and questions framed in a way that helps the team interpret and aggregate the results.

The use of computer technology at participation events is increasing. Some computer programs allow you to sketch via an electronic tablet. These methods can help stimulate discussion, with illustrations and presentations created as part of the exercise, by members of the public and/or the project team. They can also help the team to prepare workshops, especially a series of similar events with different facilitators.

2.5.3 Presenting images

The following graphic presentations
are often used for public consultation
because they are user-friendly and
readily understood.

For those not familiar with them,
two-dimensional plans can be difficult
to grasp. Three dimensions are easier.
Rendering two-dimensional images can
help, as can aerial photography. Most
people have some knowledge of maps,
however, and a familiar map format may
be appropriate for small scale plans
covering wide areas.

Vertical aerial photography

Oblique aerial photography

Vertical aerial photography with montage

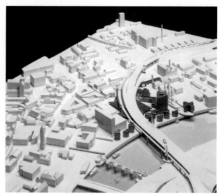

Physical model

Cartoon sketch

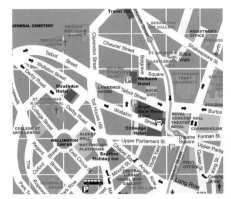

Tourist-style map clearly indicating street names and using familiar symbols

Simple computer-generated block model

Computer-generated image

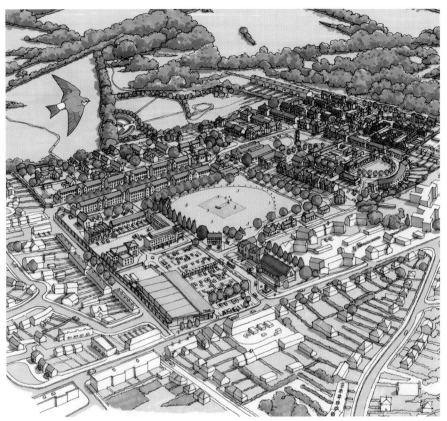

Aerial perspective

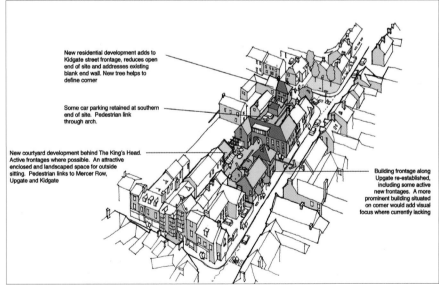

New residential development adds to Kidgate street frontage, reduces open end of site and addresses existing blank end wall. New tree helps to define corner

Some car parking retained at southern end of site. Pedestrian link through arch.

New courtyard development behind The King's Head. Active frontages where possible. An attractive enclosed and landscaped space for outside sitting. Pedestrian links to Mercer Row, Upgate and Kidgate

Building frontage along Upgate re-established, including some active new frontages. A more prominent building situated on corner would add visual focus where currently lacking

Annotated perspective sketch

Graphics in the urban design process   Chapter 2   **33**

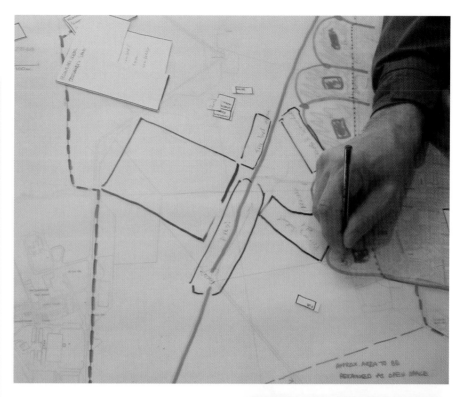

Public participation graphics:

- Most members of the public are not trained in map and plan reading. Many know their locality well but will read a map of it with difficulty. Illustrate landmarks and familiar features on maps to help people relate to them – churches, monuments, parks, schools and public art etc.

- The public generally have a strong understanding of an area; what is good, bad, works or does not work. They will need help in expressing their thoughts visually.

- Keep it simple, clear and focused on the main messages; this is not the arena for technical bravado.

- Think what covers the messages best: written lists, annotated photographs etc. Sketches may have a stronger role than plans.

- Keep plans clear and uncluttered; keys/legends, notes, scales and north points must be read easily.

- Making a simple physical block model on an Ordnance Survey© base jointly with members of the public is a worthwhile exercise where time allows.

- Use photographs, including historic photographs, if possible. Community memory can be a powerful contribution.

Materials checklist:

- All materials for drawing painting, sticking, cutting etc.

- Pens, markers, crayons all checked in advance.

- Sketch and tracing paper, acetates.

- Supplementary lighting to illuminate specific areas.

- Audio visual and recording equipment.

- Feedback forms.

- Staff t-shirts and name badges.

- Background and contextual images and photographs.

2.6
Rationale

Most projects are built around a set of key concepts and themes. These emerge during the contextual and spatial analysis and are reinforced and validated through the participation stages to shape the consequent proposals. These might include the reinforcing of the prevailing urban grain, or exploiting site topography or historic character. In locations where there is little distinction, or where the character is generally negative or degraded, new development may be an opportunity to introduce new features and characteristics to create a sense of local distinctiveness. Whichever is most appropriate, illustrative material can help pull together the existing and/or new stimuli that will ultimately determine the physical character of the completed project.

This rationale is sometimes presented as a 'storyboard' of photographs, diagrams, sketches, images and cartoons, each identifying a theme, so that the evolving project can be seen to build upon them. Whatever the style of images used, the process of setting them down in a form that can be shared is an important and essential part of the process.

The images here show how existing and new features can be presented, and how the way they are combined can inform the character of the ultimate development.

A suggested layout using photographs of existing examples (local or from elsewhere) to convey a sense of what is intended.

A photographic record of existing local buildings of character that might inform the character of new development.

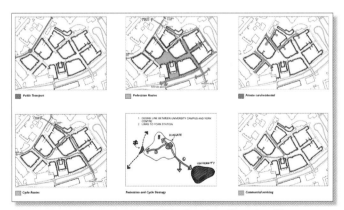

Diagrammatic representation of possibilities for a place, illustrating different elements of its future character.

2.7
Preliminary proposals

The project team will synthesise and develop the ideas generated and gathered in the rationale. Graphic techniques should concentrate on helping the various specialists to contribute to emerging options for the development. Conventions familiar to urban designers, engineers, landscape architects and other team members can short cut otherwise lengthy explanations and debate.

The principles must be clear, avoiding too much detail. A sense of 'work in progress' is important; the public and stakeholders still have a role to play in testing and validating preliminary proposals.

Working drawings to help development professionals work together will have to be presented to members of the public for their further involvement. Complex plans may have to be redrawn and simplified.

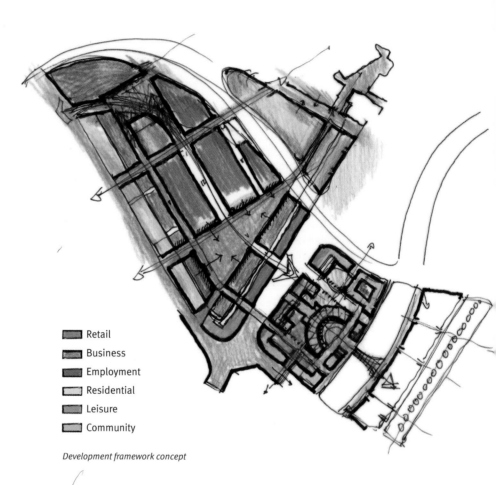

Retail
Business
Employment
Residential
Leisure
Community

Development framework concept

What it shows:

- proposed development blocks
- indicative land uses
- route structure
- key frontages.

Why it is good graphically:

- hand-drawn sketch to re-emphasise preliminary status
- contrasting colours between land uses
- development blocks emphasised with strong outlines.

2.8
Option testing

Presenting options is an important stage in project development. The range of alternatives must be presented consistently to ensure useful and reliable consultation and review. Plans, perspectives and diagrams at different scales can differentiate between the overall and the local, the general and specific. As well as illustrating what options could look like, other issues to consider illustrating include: the use of open space, traffic circulation, land uses, phasing of construction, and so on. An informal graphic style, with the options presented as simple diagrams to highlight points of difference will help focus attention on comparing elements and making choices.

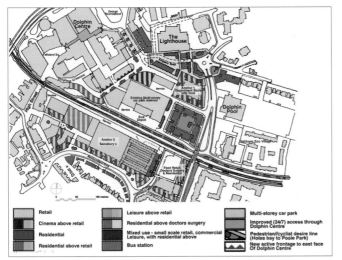

Option 1: Minimal intervention

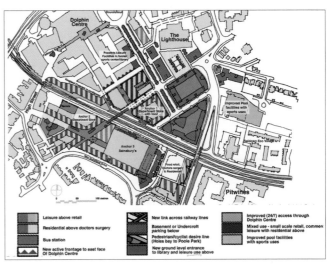

Option 2: Accessibility theme

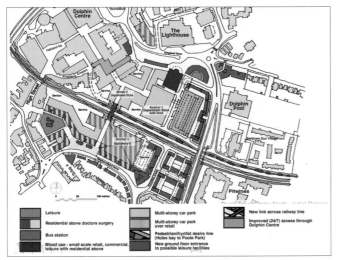

Option 3: Residential theme

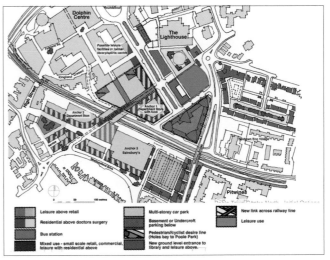

Option 4: Leisure theme

Case study 1

Vision for Scarborough

Commissioned by:
Yorkshire Forward

Consultant:
John Thompson & Partners

Challenge:
Finding and using the graphic techniques most appropriate for engaging local communities in the vision process.

New mixed use and mixed tenure building set back from existing building line to create new market square.

View along James Street towards new residential development on St Marys Hospital.

View along Columbus Road towards new mixed use landmark building.

The visioning process carried out in Scarborough is a large-scale example of community involvement, important in the development of credible regeneration strategies. Graphics play an important role in such exercises by helping facilitate discussion and communicate future possibilities.

In public workshops, participants are often reluctant to draw in front of others, and a design professional with hand-drawing skills facilitated discussions, recording information and/or design proposals suggested by members of the public. The drawings in this instance were made using coloured marker pens over scaled base material including site plans and aerial photographs. The facilitators were instructed to make their graphics large, bold and simple, with the aim of capturing not only what was discussed, but also the vitality of the brainstorming session.

Presenting the final vision back to a community required careful thought. With only a week between start and finish, the design proposals could not be fully resolved.

The hand-drawn aerial perspective was based on a specially-commissioned aerial photograph. It presents a general picture at an appropriate level of detail. The drawing required specialist skills and was executed sufficiently accurately for individual areas to be extracted and enlarged for more detailed discussion. These were paired with before and after perspectives at street level to illustrate more precisely how places well known to the audience could be transformed.

Well planned and facilitated community consultation led to a vast array of ideas from the local people that were reflected in the proposals.

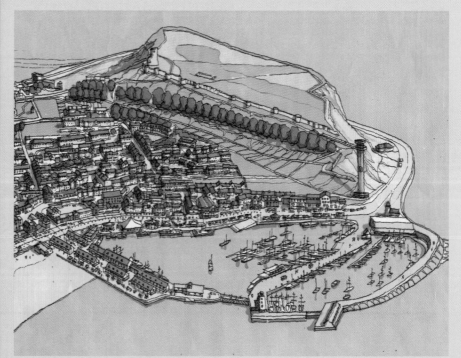

Aerial perspective created at appropriate detail

As well as physical changes, discussions on the vision for Scarborough raised issues such as the state of the economy, sectors with growth potential, and mechanisms for regeneration. While fundamental to successful urbanism, such issues are less tangible than the creation of new buildings or streetscapes. This was overcome in the presentations and subsequently by using cartoons and tourist style maps to visualise the concepts and make them more accessible to a general audience. The images employed visual metaphors, humour, and local imagery to further engage people and deepen their understanding of the overall regeneration strategy.

The disconnected town

Mending the net

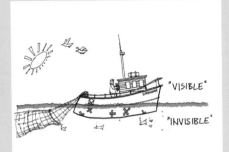

Ship-shape

Otherwise....

Festival

Investment

2.9
Final proposals

Having determined the preferred option – possibly a combination of elements from the various draft options tested – the graphics style becomes more definitive, communicating the detail of urban design and other elements of the ultimate development. This requires illustrative material and techniques that are harder, more formal and definitive. Some details may need to be measurable from the plans, such as development plot sizes, visual envelopes and heights of buildings.

2.9.1 Diagram

The main purpose of a diagram is to present or explain the organisation of elements of the development such as roads and other infrastructure, ensuring that all connections are identified and understood. Exact co-ordination with physical layout is not necessary. Diagrams can be presented as a series to avoid over-complication. Although a diagram may be drawn to the correct scale, it generally requires graphic simplicity and the removal of extraneous elements, as well as careful selection of colour and line weight to strengthen the primary message.

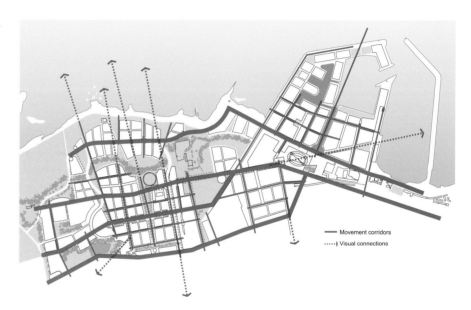

What it shows:

- basic movement pattern and hierarchy
- relationship of the development to existing waterside infrastructure
- urban grid and block structure
- visual connections.

Why it is good graphically:

- important information highlighted in bright colour
- water bodies in blue – darkest at boundary with land to emphasise the distinction
- hierarchy of routes expressed through line weight
- all extraneous detail removed
- base-map in neutral tone.

2.9.2 Masterplan

Masterplans typically include a series of themed drawings which together define the principal elements of a proposed development. These may include land use, built form, roads, communications, surface drainage, open space/landscape structure and construction phasing. The level of detail will depend on the purpose of the plan. Some are intended to stimulate development by presenting a vision; others are working documents that will guide successive stages of a commitment to development already made. Some masterplans are diagrams, explaining key development principles; others are illustrative plans, as below, portraying the indicative layout of built forms and open space. Such masterplans are typically drawn on a scaled base-plan and then rendered to make them easier to interpret.

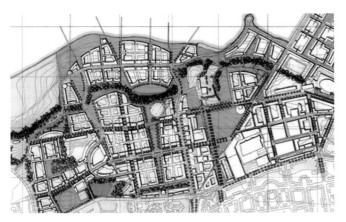

What it shows:

- indicative built form and blocking
- landscape structure
- urban grain and orientation
- overall character.

Why it is good graphically:

- proposed buildings are rendered with shadow
- all extraneous detail removed
- grid lines drawn as a device for checking scale
- existing trees distinguished by darker green
- drawn to a level of accuracy that is measurable.

2.9.3 Eye-level perspective

The hand-drawn perspective remains a very effective way of conveying the intended character and feel of places, yet to be designed in detail, as they might be experienced at street level. This can help convey the vision of what is to be achieved. It is familiar to most audiences, giving an understandable impression of what is intended without having to resolve the architectural and landscape detail. Computer generated wire-frames or photographs are often used as bases for the drawings.

What it shows:

- intended character of places
- indicative building form without detail
- atmosphere instead of architecture
- sense of scale between buildings.

Why it is good graphically:

- bright colours enhance the energy and positive atmosphere of the image
- a mix of people and uses emphasise the importance of activity to the success of the new place
- strong shadows and a blue sky giving a positive impression of a bright sunny day
- user-friendly and accessible view.

2.9.4 Aerial perspective

Aerial perspectives can bring a two-dimensional plan to life. They provide a realistic image from a high viewpoint to explain the relationship between different parts of the urban fabric, existing and proposed. In skilled hands, this form of perspective can convey the broad sweep of a masterplan, or the way in which a group of buildings will occupy their site. With careful control of detail, key areas can be emphasised and others suppressed. As with the eye-level perspective, the base for the drawing may be provided by an aerial photograph or computer-generated wire-frame.

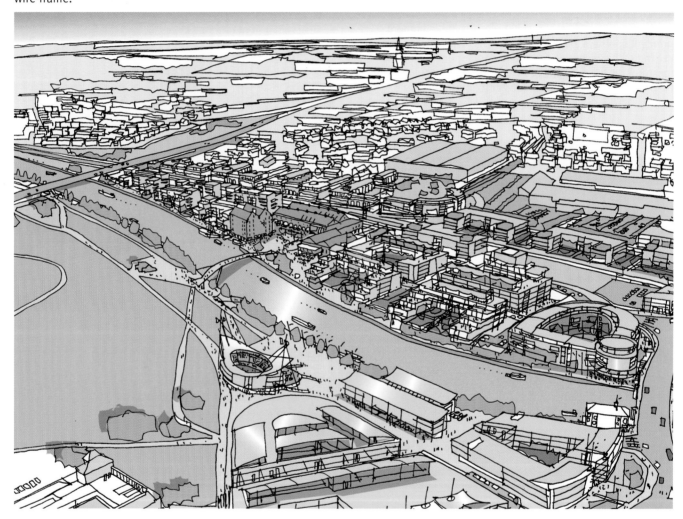

What it shows:

- realistic presentation of urban form and landscape
- places, projects and development areas in the real context
- vision of potential and long-term outcomes
- user-friendly and accessible overview.

Why it is good graphically:

- colours stronger in the foreground and weaker in the background
- minimal colour palette used to differentiate general topography and buildings
- consistent use of colour palette and effective use of tints
- reflective surfaces i.e. water, banded with a white streak.

2.9.5 Axonometric

This is a three-dimensional projection
constructed from a scale plan set at an
angle, usually 45°, with buildings drawn
to the same scale across the drawing
(therefore, without perspective).
Although it lacks the more realistic
impression of an aerial perspective,
the axonometric is easily and quickly
constructed, and is a straightforward
way of presenting buildings and spaces
in relation to each other. The illusion of
depth can be enhanced by emboldening
the leading edges of buildings and
suppressing detail towards the edge
of the drawing.

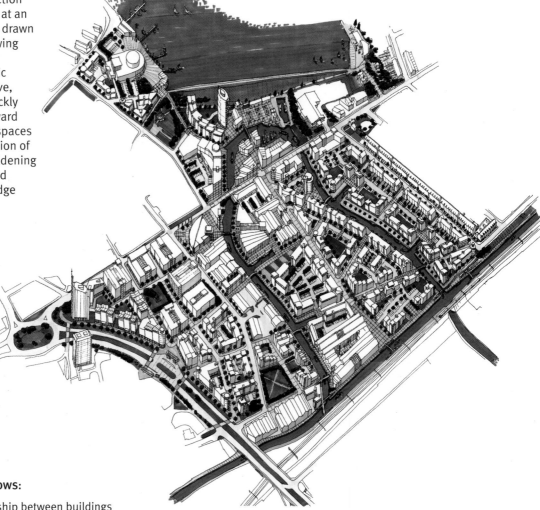

What it shows:

- relationship between buildings
  and spaces
- indicative built form and massing
- overall character of proposals
  rather than detail.

Why it is good graphically:

- appropriate colours to show
  both hard (tan) and soft (green)
  landscaping
- pattern and colour used together
  to depict different surfaces, e.g.
  shared or pedestrian surfaces
- water bodies, green spaces, trees
  and spaces between buildings
  coloured, leaving built form to
  stand out.

2.9.6 Map/plan

Maps are the most familiar form of geographic information and are often used as a basis for preparing presentations. The information they contain and the way it is presented make them user-friendly and easy for audiences to understand.

What it shows:

- geographic information
- correct scale relationship between elements
- information in familiar and accessible form.

Why it is good graphically:

- conventional and familiar colours used to differentiate elements
- all extraneous detail removed from base-map
- drawn to scale, providing base for proposals.

2.9.7 3-D computer block model

This is an image which corresponds to a view of a physical model, showing a section of urban fabric or landscape in perspective from above. It is usually generated upwards from a scale plan with additional information added, often photo-enhanced with detail adjusted to focus on the key elements of the project. With the bespoke computer programs now available, alternative urban forms, different density and building form options can be rapidly modelled and presented as an aid to audience understanding, without needing to design the buildings in detail.

What it shows:

- scale and massing
- relationships between buildings and spaces
- overall development pattern.

Why it is good graphically:

- good contrast between proposed and existing
- water bodies shown in blue, landscaping in green and development in brown
- angle of aerial view selected to best convey the scheme.

2.9.8 3-D computer detail model

Computer-generated images of buildings and spaces can achieve high levels of realism through increasingly sophisticated modelling techniques, which allow viewpoints, lighting conditions and architectural detail to be varied according to the purpose of the presentation.

What it shows:

- surface materials and planting scheme
- architecture in detail
- pedestrian and shared surfaces.

Why it is good graphically:

- shadows cast for greater reality
- realistic sky
- people proportioned accurately in relation to buildings
- glazed areas show reflections.

2.9.9 Cartoon

There are cases where a broad planning concept can best be expressed through a loose freehand sketch or cartoon. These can sometimes gain greater importance as an icon of the project. Cartoons have no scale or geographic base. They are essentially fresh and spontaneous in character, presenting key relationships rather than precise information, either singly or as a set of images conveying project themes.

What it shows:

- key themes and topics
- concepts and messages
- talking points – consultation
- response to very local issues
- uses humour to emphasise the message (make sure the humour does not reinforce community cynicism).

Why it is good graphically:

- clearly depicted as an anecdote
- drawing style consistent with the humour
- not over-specific on location.

2.9.10 Elevation

When included in planning presentations, conventional architectural elevations are a very effective way of explaining existing or intended streetscape. They can show scale, character, materials and detailing, especially that of a terrace, cluster or group of buildings in their context. Hand-drawn elevations traced over a scale base are a common form of presentation, conveying a softer, more informal feel.

What it shows:

- key elements of design
- relative scale and massing
- intended character
- heights and proportions.

Why it is good graphically:

- shadows emphasise modelling of building
- minimal colour palette used
- glazing distinguished from other materials
- presents realistic proportions and relationships.

2.9.11 Section

Illustrative sections through buildings and spaces, especially when they include a variety of uses arranged vertically, help explain the relationship between these uses in context. They can explain how internal spaces spill out into the public realm, how the profile of a building responds to its setting or the flexibility to change uses over time. Even a simple sketch section can help explain the complexities of levels, especially on a sloping site or when levels are split.

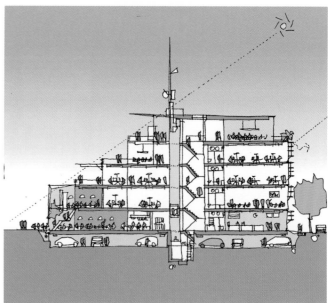

What it shows:

- vertical stacking of uses
- relationship of building(s) to public realm
- building heights and proportions
- roof profiles and skylines.

Why it is good graphically:

- contrasting colours to emphasise different elements
- presents realistic proportions and relationships
- people and cars included to give instant sense of scale.

2.9.12 Design code drawings

Illustrations for design code documents should express key concepts in a way that is readily understood by non-specialists as well as by the professional teams involved in designing new developments.

They typically include diagrams defining the design parameters for layout and buildings.

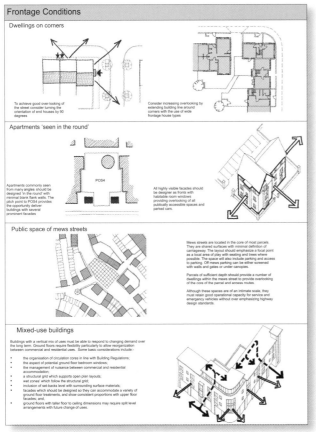

Extract from a design code document

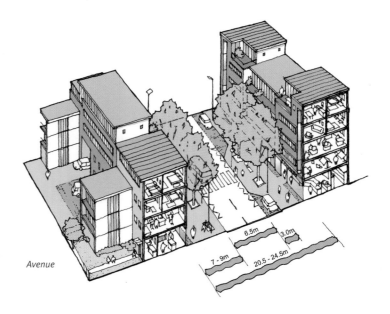

Avenue

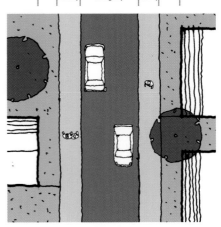

Local street

2.9.13 Photomontage

This is the technique of merging drawn or other images with photography.

It can help present the reality of the existing context as the setting for new buildings or public realm. The technique is particularly useful in demonstrating the visual impact proposals would have on the existing environment and showing people how a place will be transformed. The effect can be achieved manually or by using computer or digital camera software.

Watchpoints

- Use colours on the drawing that complement the photograph.

- Perspective must be accurate to the aerial photograph or images will appear distorted.

- Ensure the cut-out, real or virtual, is an accurate fit on the site.

- Make sure drawing and photograph are of equal resolution.

- Blur and make edge semi-transparent to produce a smooth transition between drawing and photograph.

Step 1: Obtain aerial photograph

Step 2: Sketch the aerial perspective over the photograph

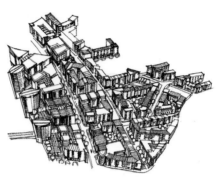

Step 3: Clean up perspective sketch and add final details

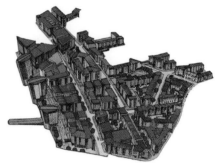

Step 4: Add colour to the sketch

Blurring edges and making them semi-transparent where the coloured perspective meets the photograph produces a smooth transition.

Step 5: Scan and digitally montage aerial perspective onto the photograph and adjust overall colour balance

Photomontage can also be used to enhance particular elements of an image, such as replacing an overcast or uninteresting sky with something more attractive. A good match between the new material and the background is essential for a realistic and convincing modified image, taking into account lighting conditions, perspective, angle of view and shadows cast.

Correct scaling of objects is important. Any human figures inserted must be correctly sized according to their position in the perspective. Any anomalies will be immediately obvious to the eye and the composition will lose credibility. Accuracy of cast shadows is also important.

When accurately and honestly constructed, photomontages can be powerful advocates for urban design projects, especially if the 3-D modelling of the new proposals has been skillfully managed to ensure a seamless blend with the photographic background.

Original photo has a dull sky

Superimposed sky to improve background

Correct scaling of human figures according to perspective

2.9.14 Before-and-after

With increasingly sophisticated computer packages, photomontage is a good way of showing before-and-after images of new development proposals. Very precise representations of a proposal can help evaluate the impact. However, a rigorous and auditable set-up procedure is vital to ensure images are not over manipulated or distorted in a way that would misrepresent what exists and/or the impact of the proposals.

Hand-drawn images of the proposed development can be paired with the original photograph to emphasise particular characteristics.

Before: Original photograph

After: Computer-generated model photomontaged onto original photograph

The computer model shows the architecture in detail

Before: Panoramic photography stitched together

After: Hand-drawn sketch coloured in a computer package

The hand-drawn sketch depicts overall project proposals and atmosphere

2.9.15 Accurate visual representation (AVR)

AVRs are prepared by combining images generated from a three-dimensional computer model of the proposals with their context. The level of detail now available in computer-generated images requires measures to verify their accuracy and honesty.

There is an emerging classification for AVRs which is essentially a sliding scale in which each stage incorporates all the properties of the previous stage plus additional information building the level of realism.

The following categories are proposed as a useful working guide to the information and visual properties of each distinct level of presentation.

AVR0 - showing size and location

Type	Visual properties defined	Typical forms of presentation
AVR0	Location and size of proposal	Silhouette generated from simple massing model of proposals superimposed onto a photograph or video sequence.
AVR1	Location, size and visibility of proposal	Silhouette generated from simple massing model of proposals superimposed onto a photograph or video sequence – line omitted, dotted or shaded where obscured by existing structures.
AVR2	Location, size, visibility and architectural form	Photo- or video-montage based on simple shaded renderings from computer models which depict important architectural details of façade and roofscape, without distinguishing between materials.
AVR3	Location, size, visibility, architectural form and use of materials	Photo- or video-montage combining renderings from detailed computer models which depict façade, roofscape and relevant interior details. Proposed materials are depicted using either schematic or artistic treatments in response to an indicative lighting scenario.

AVR1 - showing degree of visibility

While these definitions and the images opposite refer to the creation of accurately executed photo- or video-montage, AVRs can also be generated by combining models of proposals with accurate models of their context.

AVR2 - explaining architectural form

AVR3 - explaining form and use of materials

Case Study 2

Brierley Hill, Dudley Borough, West Midlands

Commissioned by:
Chelsfield plc
Dudley Metropolitan Borough Council

Consultant:
David Lock Associates

Challenge:
Using graphic design to help convey and promote an ambitious vision for radical re-structuring of an urban area and translate that vision into a clear policy framework and supplementary planning guidance on implementation.

Since the mid-1990s, the owner of the Merry Hill Shopping Centre has been working in partnership with Dudley Metropolitan Borough Council to transform the area around and including Merry Hill into a new town centre. The strategy is entirely without precedent within the UK and highly innovative in terms of both physical masterplanning and policy development.

Graphic design has played a vital role in conveying often complicated and challenging concepts to a range of different audiences in the early stages:

- Plan-based diagrams and concept plans were used to explain the area and opportunities.

- The initial masterplan and layered diagrams explained the approach to land use, transportation, character and public realm. (The graphic technique employed emphasised key principles without being too geographically specific or alluding to architectural form and mass).

- The aerial perspective demonstrated how the design principles might be applied, helping the public to understand the more abstract elements of the urban design agenda and raising aspirations about the quality of the place.

The Area Development Framework, which set out the initial strategy for change, won a Royal Town Planning Institute award for Urban Design in 1999. The graphic content was particularly commended.

Translation of the strategy into policy demanded a very different graphic interpretation; the essential elements of the masterplan were translated into a Development Plan proposals map.

As the project progressed, the masterplan was refined to serve a number of different purposes. Commercial land use proposals emerged for many of the available development opportunities across the study area. The revised masterplan brought these together to give a complete picture of the development potential through accurate representation of built form and the public realm. The level of precision allowed built development to be quantified, individual projects defined and infrastructure costs apportioned. In this way the plan formed the basis of an implementation strategy.

Aerial perspective showing the initial impression of the new town centre

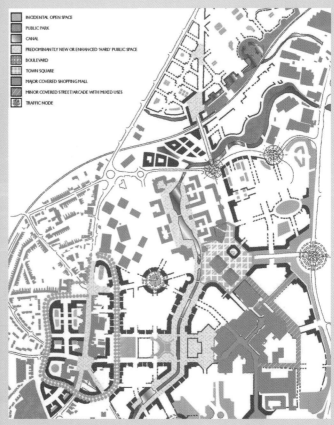

Initial masterplan – public realm diagram showing key development principles

INCIDENTAL OPEN SPACE
PUBLIC PARK
CANAL
PREDOMINANTLY NEW OR ENHANCED 'HARD' PUBLIC SPACE
BOULEVARD
TOWN SQUARE
MAJOR COVERED SHOPPING MALL
MINOR COVERED STREET/ARCADE WITH MIXED USES
TRAFFIC NODE

The masterplan remains an important promotional tool. It is attractively coloured and rendered using drop shadows (to give a sense of the scale of the buildings) and including details within the public realm (including vehicles, people, landscaping and surface materials) to convey scale and character.

A new aerial perspective, rendered using a digital paint program. The image has also been made into a three-dimensional fly-through, used extensively for public consultation and marketing investment opportunities.

Refined masterplan – accurate representation of plan form and definition of the public realm

Aerial perspective of Lower Brierley showing massing, varied architectural forms and integration of new and established uses

2.10
Presenting details

In many projects there are details of the final proposals that have to be particularly presented because they will inform further work, possibly by others. Accuracy, clarity and ease of interpretation are paramount.

2.10.1 Footpaths and cycleways

This shows footpaths and cycleways in relation to the places and spaces they serve – open spaces, parks, public transport etc. Information is presented as broken lines on a generalised map-base. Lines are not to scale as they would appear too narrow. Footpaths and cycleways are generally coloured green. When showing separate cycleways and pedestrian routes, complementary colours are required.

Devonport, Plymouth

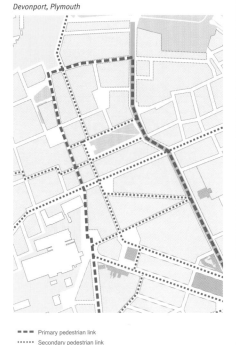

- - - Primary pedestrian link
······· Secondary pedestrian link
▬▬ Cycleway

What it shows:

- network of routes
- hierarchy and importance
- grain of network
- relationship to road/street network.

Why it is good graphically:

- footpaths shown in a green broken line
- cycleways shown in a complementary colour
- all extraneous detail removed.

2.10.2 Building heights

Height is often represented by the number of floors of each building block and the distribution of building heights across the scheme. This information can be presented on a base-map or a figure ground as keyed categories or by annotation onto each zone.

Bere Hill, Andover

▬ 4 storeys
▬ 3 storeys
▬ 2 storeys

What it shows:

- hierarchy of building heights
- gradations and points of change
- points of emphasis through building height.

Why it is good graphically:

- hierarchy of colour – strongest colour expressing greatest height
- all extraneous detail removed.

2.10.3 Road/street types

Plans portray the hierarchy of streets within the built form and urban environment. This is presented as a series of lines representing the road/street type and hierarchy, the colours graded in terms of the road/street types.

South Bank, Peterborough

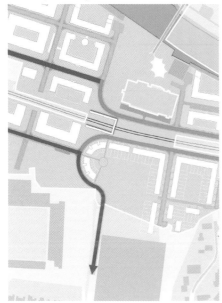

—— Major street
—— General street
—— Local street

2.10.4 Density

This plan illustrates an existing or proposed range of residential densities as part of an area study or masterplan. It is generally presented as a graded range of colours or tones on a base-plan to indicate bands of density, with higher densities made the most prominent.

Waterfront Granton, Edinburgh

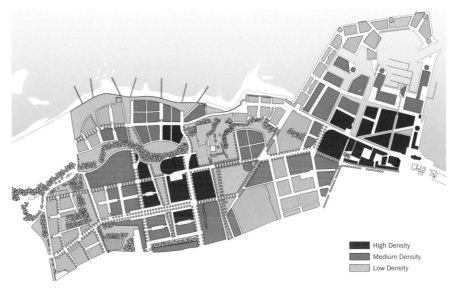

■ High Density
■ Medium Density
□ Low Density

What it shows:

- network of routes
- road/street hierarchy
- grain of network
- relationship to building frontages.

Why it is good graphically:

- clearly shows hierarchy of streets through use of colour
- development detail suppressed to focus attention on road hierarchy.

What it shows:

- range of densities
- gradations and points of change
- relationship to open space/ public realm.

Why it is good graphically:

- hierarchy of colour – strongest colour expressing highest density
- all extraneous detail removed
- base-map in neutral colour.

2.10.5 Nodes

These emphasise points of greater intensity of activity, the connections between them and the convergence of routes. They are usually presented as a network of bold circles ranked in order of intensity of activity at nodes and along routes, on a base-map or figure ground.

Chancery Lane, London

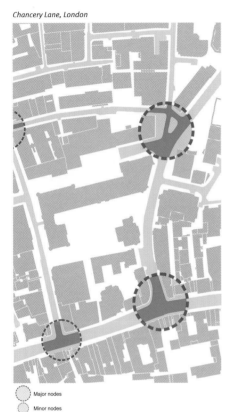

Major nodes

Minor nodes

What it shows:

- hierarchy of nodes
- relationship to road/street hierarchy
- relationship to built form.

Why it is good graphically:

- colour contrast between routes and nodes
- hierarchy of nodes shown through size
- converging routes highlighted within nodes
- all irrelevant detail suppressed
- figure ground in neutral colour.

2.10.6 Land use

Plans identify the uses to be ascribed to discrete plots of land across the study area, usually on a base-map. At larger scales, additional plans may be required to indicate different uses on different floor levels within the development.

Devonport, Plymouth

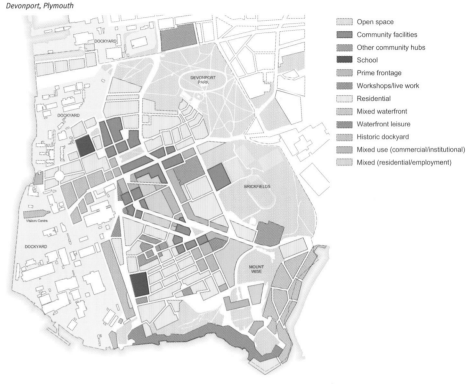

Open space
Community facilities
Other community hubs
School
Prime frontage
Workshops/live work
Residential
Mixed waterfront
Waterfront leisure
Historic dockyard
Mixed use (commercial/institutional)
Mixed (residential/employment)

What it shows:

- land use categories
- relationship between uses
- relationship to road/street hierarchy.

Why it is good graphically:

- contrasting colours used to distinguish different land uses
- distinguishes between existing and proposed development
- boundary shows extent of the study area.

2.10.7 Active frontages

These plans indicate the relatively higher intensity of activity that will be generated by shops, public uses and building entrances at street level. Information is often presented on a map or figure ground with the strength of lines or colour indicating levels of activity.

Chancery Lane, London

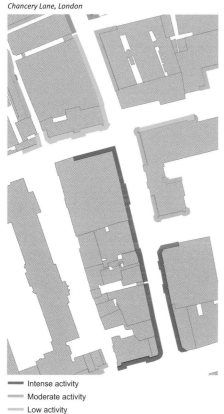

▬ Intense activity
▬ Moderate activity
▬ Low activity

2.10.8 Public transport network

Plans identify routes/stops/frequency of bus/tram/rail services and interchange on an area plan, sometimes including zones based on standard walking times from the public transport corridor. Differentiated lines represent the different modes of transport. Standard symbols are used for the stops or stations. A base-map sets the services provided in the wider urban context, indicating the level of penetration of services and their accessibility.

Nottingham

━● NET & Stops ━━ Other Main Roads
●●●● City Centre Bus Loop ◉ New Transport Interchange
━━ City Centre relief route ▨ Traffic reduction

What it shows:

- hierarchy of importance
- points of change and intensity
- relationship to built form.

Why it is good graphically:

- shows hierarchy of frontages through use of colour
- all extraneous detail removed.

What it shows:

- public transport modes
- urban structure and road network
- main interchange and stops.

Why it is good graphically:

- clear distinction between the different public transport modes
- all extraneous detail removed
- base-map in neutral colour.

2.10.9 Phasing plan

Most large urban planning projects require illustrations of the intended sequence of development, or phasing. This can be presented either as a standard 2-D phasing diagram or very effectively as a set of computer-generated 3-D block diagrams sequentially adding a further development phase.

Waterfront Granton, Edinburgh

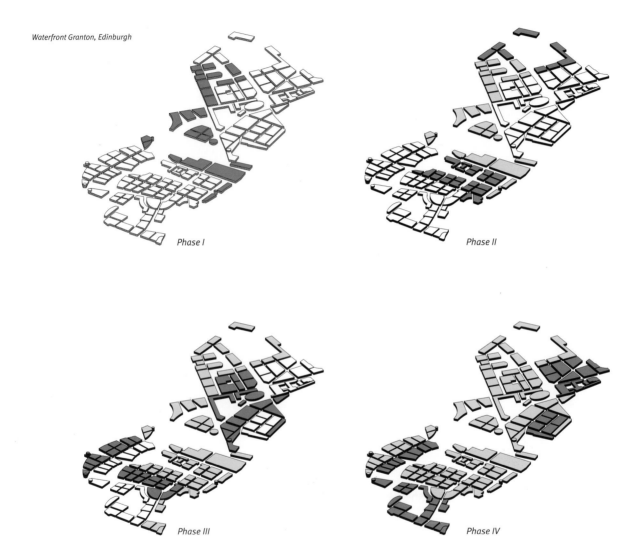

Phase I

Phase II

Phase III

Phase IV

What it shows:

- sequence of development
- incremental build up of phases
- interfaces between phases.

Why it is good graphically:

- development simplified to block model
- strong colour used to emphasise each phase
- sequential build up shown through colour tint.

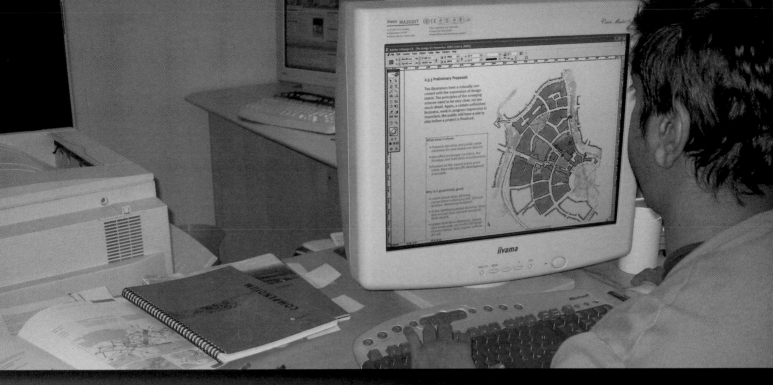

Good technical practice

chapter 3

3.1 Graphical language | 3.2 Base-maps | 3.3 Using computers |
3.4 Synergy of styles | 3.5 Desktop publishing (DTP) | 3.6 Software

This chapter addresses:

- The characteristics of drawings and illustrations that make them easy to understand.

- Illustration techniques – although there are few firm rules in the language of urban design graphics, the examples in this chapter reflect conventions that have evolved over time because they work.

- Computer programs – all have a principal purpose and should be used accordingly.

3.1
Graphical language

There are four fundamental elements that are included in plans to help us understand, orientate and interpret them. In urban design projects we will seldom find illustrations fully explained without the use of a:

- key
- title block
- north point
- scale.

Other graphic devices will aid communication, but should be used consistently and following graphic or more widely understood conventions. For example, most people in urban design will understand the difference between contour and boundary lines. When combined on a single plan there should be no chance of confusion or misinterpretation of what is depicted. The same applies to the use of colour, shading and annotation.

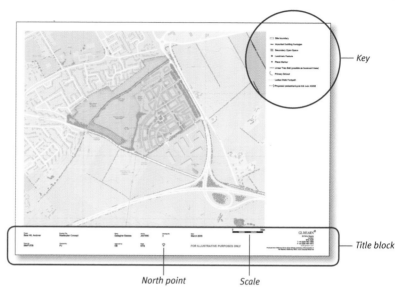

Key

Title block

North point   Scale

3.1.1 Key

It is vital to provide keys or legends, particularly on drawings when the information is not self-explanatory.

3.1.2 Title block

The title block establishes the authority of the plan or drawing. It should provide information about the author and owner, as well as the drawing itself. Drawings and plans may have a legal status and responsibility must be recorded. A title block should have the following information:

- drawing title
- drawing reference number
- the author
- the body taking responsibility
- scale (both written and drawn)
- date created
- revision number
- project codes.

All plans and drawings should be attributable and have a reliable point of reference. Clear layout and legible completion of added information are therefore essential.

3.1.3 North point

The north point should always appear on drawings. It is useful for establishing aspect and shadow paths but mainly for ensuring that all concerned orientate all drawings the right way up.

There are effectively three types of north:

- **True north** – the direction of a meridian of longitude which converges on the North Pole
- **Magnetic north** – the direction indicated by a magnetic compass. Magnetic north moves slowly with a variable rate and currently is west of grid north in Great Britain
- **Grid north** – the direction of a grid line which is parallel to the central meridian on the Ordnance Survey© grid.

The UK convention is to use grid north. It is good practice to orientate plans with north at the top. Keep the orientation simple and consistent with other related drawings.

The north point is traditionally a decorative as well as a functional graphic device. The style may be used to reflect that of the project or the team, but it should always be obvious what it is.

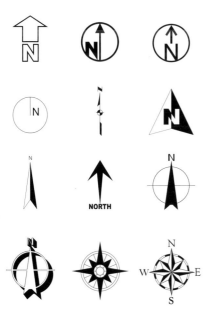

3.1.4 Scale

The scale is a ratio used to represent actual size. Scaled drawings allow different levels of detail to be presented on similarly sized plans. There are three ways to show scale:

- numeric/written scale (1:100)
- scale bar
- grid lines.

Whenever possible the scale should be included on a drawing. The following scales are typically used in mapping and urban design.

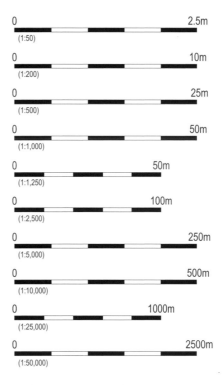

Grid lines are normally set at intervals of 50m, 100m or 1000m. The example below shows grid lines at intervals of 100m at a scale of 1:50,000.

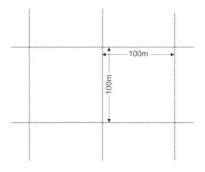

3.1.5 Site location

Three different graphic techniques for indicating site location on both aerial photography and base-map are shown below.

Outline

Shade

Outline and mask

Watchpoints

- Do not use lines similar in colour or type to delineate different boundaries.

- Site boundaries are commonly shown in red.

- Follow precise boundaries in accordance with land parcels and ownerships.

3.1.6 Boundaries

Boundaries are an essential component of a plan – differentiating between discrete areas. The form of the line that marks out the boundary should be appropriate to what it is enclosing, and should be clearly different from lines on the plan setting out baseline information on existing landform and structures.

Boundaries can be:

Definitive – showing precise alignment of boundaries. These are normally shown as solid lines and usually shown in red (if highlighting a site) unless this conflicts with other information.

Indicative – depicting general areas with broken lines that do not commit to precision and tend to be a series of curved rather than straight lines.

3.1.7 Arrows

Arrows are used to depict direction – of movement, of view, of sun path for example – but may also be used to point to key features in or beyond the plan. It is better to avoid using both on the same plan, but if this is essential then the forms of the arrows should be distinct and explained in the key. Arrows should be designed so that their outline cannot be confused with elements of the base plan.

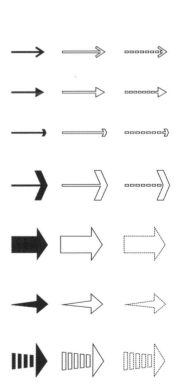

3.1.8 Line weights/types

Lines can also represent paths, movement or links. A hierarchy of lines can be established by:

- width
- tone
- type.

The width of such lines can be used to represent the level of activity along a particular route. The tone of a line can be depicted by colour or shade and used to depict significance or emphasis. The type of a line – the relative interval of solid and space – can be used to depict levels of confidence or the provisional or conditional nature of what is depicted.

Weight	Tone	Type

3.1.9 Logo

Logos are used to brand projects, organisations and products and to create a unique, consistent image. They should be easily identified and act as a memorable signature. They can play a vital role in marketing and promoting urban projects. However abstract, they should in some way reflect or respond to the subject. Those responsible should ensure that it cannot be misinterpreted, confused with another or offer opportunities for misuse. Logos are generally created from type and/or symbols.

The type describes the organisation through its company name and strap line. The graphic mark/symbol represents the four main bridges that cross the Great River Ouse in Bedford and the colour blue is used to represent water.

The graphic mark/symbol represents the physical structure of Oxford City Centre divided into quarters and the West End quarter is further sub-divided, symbolised by the bright magenta against the neutral stone colour of historic Oxford. The modern typeface and bright colours used throughout the branding help to communicate the forward-looking development proposals.

3.1.10 Layering

Separate layers of information can be presented on a common base-map to aid analysis of different issues or themes relating to a proposal. This reduces clutter and avoids confusion. They can be presented on both 2-D or 3-D plans. The examples below show a masterplan delayered and presented as single themes. Presenting them separately on an identical base-map allows easy comparison. Once issues are resolved it may be possible to incorporate multiple features on a single plan. This will be easier if they have been prepared to a common base.

Series of themed plans for Granton Waterfront, Edinburgh

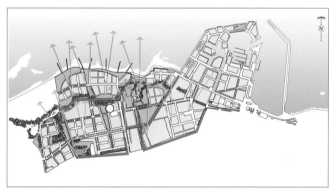

Site terraces

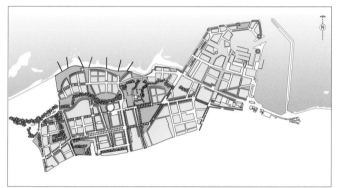

Key frontages

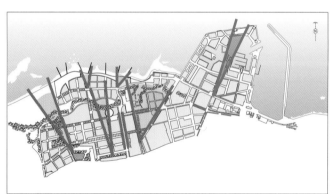

Green wedges

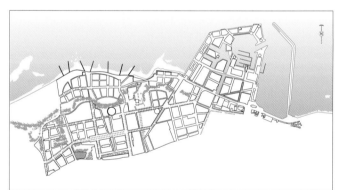

Tree-lined avenues

3.1.11 Annotation

Annotation conveys additional information that cannot easily be presented by keys or graphics alone, typically when describing sites or development opportunities. Too much annotation will obscure the message to be conveyed by the image. If extensive annotation seems inevitable, separate explanatory text with clear references to the plan may be more appropriate.

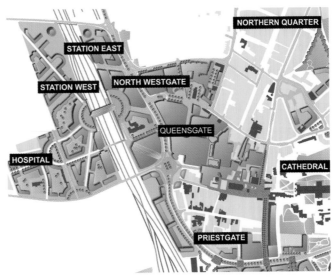

Annotation on top of a drawing obscures information and can look clumsy

Watchpoints

- Text should be as concise as possible and set in short lines.

- Text outside the frame of the figure must be clearly and accurately arrowed to the relevant location.

- Text font must be legible even if this means reducing the scale of the figure in order to create sufficient space.

- Align/justify or range the text consistently.

- Align annotation horizontally along one or two lines, avoiding staggering and scattering.

- Use abbreviations carefully, as they may be unfamiliar to users and misinterpreted.

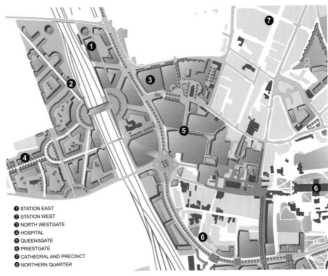

1. STATION EAST
2. STATION WEST
3. NORTH WESTGATE
4. HOSPITAL
5. QUEENSGATE
6. PRIESTGATE
7. CATHEDRAL AND PRECINCT
8. NORTHERN QUARTER

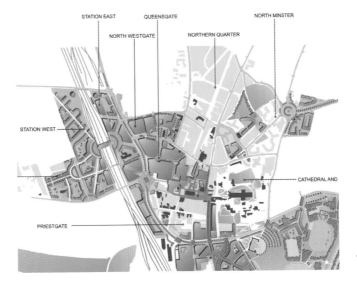

3.1.12 Symbols and graphic shorthand

As the theory and practice of urban design have matured, so too has the graphic language used to express the elements of townscape. While not being formal conventions, some symbols have come to represent specific conditions, such as a zigzag to express a noise-source or barriers to movement; lines with arrowheads to denote a direction of expansion or views. These and others have become common currency among urban designers.

Individuals and organisations devise their own ways of expressing symbols on drawings. The example opposite has been derived from traditional symbols. Some are consistent with Ordnance Survey© and others have been developed over time by urban designers.

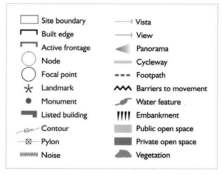

Key taken from a generic urban design analysis diagram

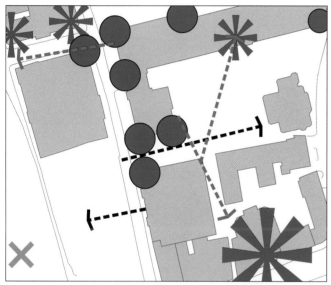

Incorrect scale and overlapping symbols have created a very cluttered diagram

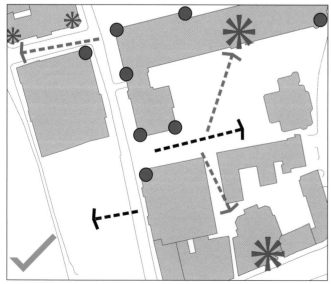

Sensible use of symbols produces a clear concise diagram

Watchpoints

- Symbols should be graphically distinct from each other.

- Symbols should be of a size that does not dominate or confuse the figure.

- Symbols need 'breathing space'; they should not clash or overlap.

- Rather than crowd a single figure with symbols, consider making points on several smaller figures with a common base so that the composite message can be more easily read.

- Keeping the size, colour and line weight of symbols consistent aids legibility.

- Use symbols where shading or lines cannot convey the message effectively.

- Symbols can indicate objects on a plan which are too small to show in detail.

- Symbols can signify commonly occurring locations or activities (such as landmarks).

3.1.13 Contours

Contours are lines on a map that connect points of the same value. They most often indicate height (altitude), but may also be used to identify other relative values, such as distance in time from a particular point (isochrones) or noise levels from a particular source. They are normally depicted in fine brown or black lines with contour annotation orientated in the direction of the incline. Intervals at which the contours are shown depend on the scale.

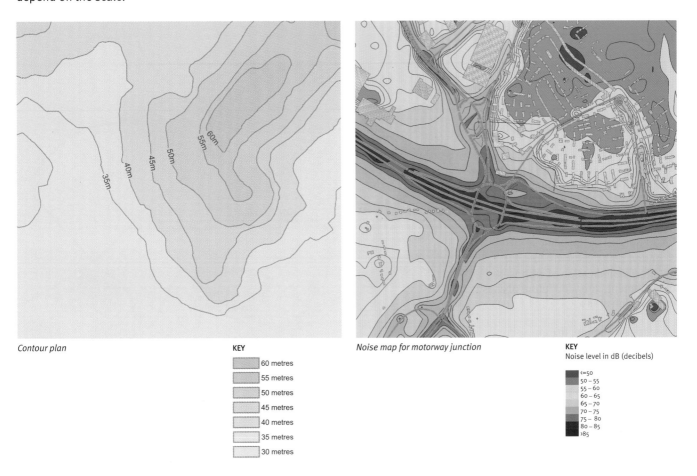

Contour plan

KEY

	60 metres
	55 metres
	50 metres
	45 metres
	40 metres
	35 metres
	30 metres

Noise map for motorway junction

KEY
Noise level in dB (decibels)

	<=50
	50 – 55
	55 – 60
	60 – 65
	65 – 70
	70 – 75
	75 – 80
	80 – 85
	>85

3.1.14 Tone, texture and pattern

Tone describes the relative lightness or darkness of a colour or shade. In graphics practice, tones can be exploited to great effect, notably when it is necessary to use a single colour. When several colours are used, lighter and darker tones provide a means of differentiating graphically a hierarchy of values or relative degrees of intensity.

Textures can add depth and grain to areas on a plan where a more three-dimensional effect is required. They work particularly well in denoting areas such as woodland or rough terrain, distinguishing them from built form and surfaces which are expressed with smooth colour.

Patterns are generally used to delineate areas without definitive boundaries. Unlike textures, they do not create a depth or grain and can work well as an overlay to existing base information. Whether used as hatching, mesh or dotted areas, patterns can give an effective indication of proposed development, intended future phases or extension areas.

Used together, tone, texture and pattern add emphasis and energy to a plan, but it takes practice to combine them successfully and prevent the message being swamped by too many combinations.

Tone, texture and pattern working together illustrating west Milton Keynes transport corridor

Green shade varying in tone illustrating open areas

Textured area depicting trees and woodland

Pattern illustrating future development area/corridor

Patterns

Textures

Most monotone patterns should not obscure information layered below

Examples that express surface grain or texture

Watchpoints

- Use tone to delineate large continuous areas.

- Use textures to give an appearance of surface qualities e.g. woodland or rough terrain.

- Use patterns to delineate approximate areas that can be overlaid without obscuring information below.

3.1.15 Existing and proposed

Proposals must be distinct and clearly differentiated from the existing urban fabric. A clear and confident presentation will ensure that the audience understands what is proposed.

Watchpoints

- Use neutral or light colours for the existing base-map.

- Show the proposals in bolder or brighter colours.

- Remove detail from the existing base-map.

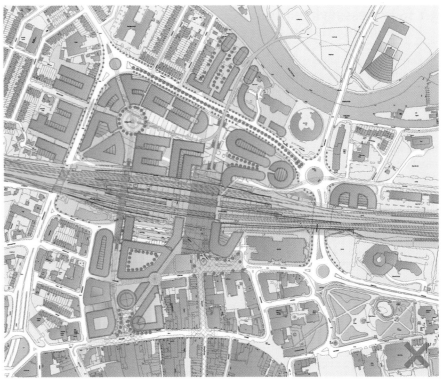

Reading station: graphically shows no contrast between existing and proposed and the base-map obscures the message with unnecessary detail

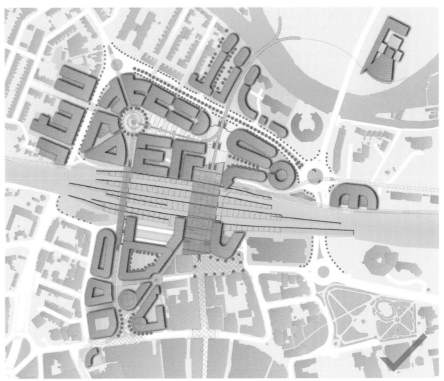

Proposals are graphically bolder and darker to differentiate existing from proposed and all extraneous detail removed from the base-map

3.1.16 Expressing intensity and importance

The relative intensity or importance of a particular activity or variable can be expressed on a plan using a ranked scale to help interpret the implications of geographically-based data. Conventionally this is achieved by graduated shade or tone, with the most intense – or important – being expressed with the deepest or most solid colour. The graduation of colour should be balanced to ensure divisions are distinct enough to read independently and that the figure is not overwhelmed by the darkest tone where the most intense or important predominates in terms of area.

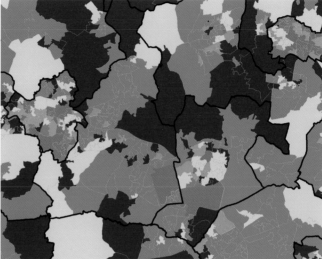

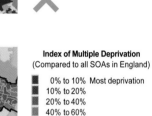

Colours conflict as well as having no logical order or hierarchy

Watchpoints

- Too many graduations may become difficult to differentiate.

- White can also be used as the lowest level.

- Print out in greyscale to check tonal difference – if it works in black and white it will work in colour.

- Use outlines to emphasise boundaries.

Colours have a logical graduation and tonal hierarchy

3.1.17 Colour logic

The standard land use colours established in post-war town planning in Britain are still widely applied, but modern colour palettes for presentations are largely a matter of individual taste. Practices and agencies will tend to develop their own preferences and some may have established house styles that influence a project's graphics. There are, however, certain commonsense applications of colour, such as greens generally denoting soft landscape and planting, blues indicating water bodies, and darker, solid colours being associated with built form or building footprints. These are not hard and fast conventions, but to move away from them to more exotic colour ranges can confuse the message to the general public.

A colour palette should be used consistently across the whole range of images for a project, reinforcing its identity and aiding cross-referencing. These colours must work successfully at all scales, so that a given figure is equally balanced as a graphic image, whether within a leaflet or on an exhibition panel, where viewing distance can be critical.

	RESIDENTIAL		LEISURE
	COMMERCIAL		LOCAL CENTRES
	INDUSTRY		HEALTH
	EMPLOYMENT		MIXED USE
	RETAIL		WATER
	EDUCATION		OPEN SPACE

An example of one palette of colours to represent land uses

3.1.18 Black and white images

Computer and printing technology allows us to use colour as easily as black and white. Messages presented in black and white, and shades of grey, may however be easier to understand, and certainly easier and cheaper to copy.

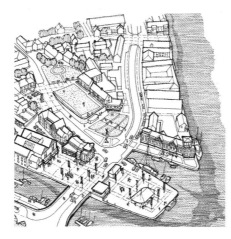

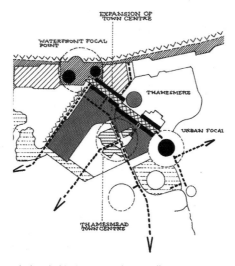

Black and white images can be very effective and should be encouraged when appropriate

Watchpoints

In selecting the most appropriate way of presenting an urban design concept graphically:

- The level of detail and style of image chosen must be determined by the message and not vice versa.

- Broad concepts need illustrative graphics rather than false precision.

- Diagrams successful at a large scale may not work as well when substantially reduced, while diagrams enlarged often read well.

- A sequence of diagrams using a simple common base is highly effective in conveying the individual themes or components of a masterplan.

- The freshest and most telling graphic presentations usually combine a mixture of graphic styles.

- Plans or diagrams at different scales and levels of detail are easier to compare and cross-relate if they contain common reference points and are presented with the same orientation.

- The intensity of detail can be varied across a plan to focus attention on what is most important.

Case Study 3

Urban realm strategy, Aberdeen

Commissioned by:
Aberdeen City Centre Partnership
Aberdeen City Council
Scottish Enterprise Grampian

Consultant:
Gillespies

Challenge:
To prepare an urban design and development strategy for a city centre; presenting options for how places could change in an understandable and accessible way.

In 2001, Aberdeen published an ambitious strategy for a fine city founded on an expansive and integrated vision for the future of the city centre. This drew inspiration from comparable cities in the UK and Europe to shape aspirations and prioritise projects to give the city centre an internationally competitive urban heart.

A key aspect of the work was the ability to communicate the challenges to be faced in order to confront the issues and bring about the necessary change.

The various media used to communicate this project to a wide ranging audience including non-professionals

The project involved the preparation of an illustrated report using hand-drawn sketches to depict the different approaches to place-making that underpinned the strategy.

Alternative approaches were examined and brought to life through sequences of sketches using the 'serial vision' technique originally developed by Gordon Cullen to 'walk people through' the possibilities for the spaces.

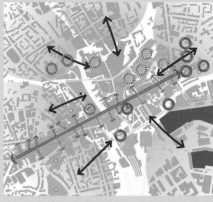

Strategy diagram showing linkages to key project areas

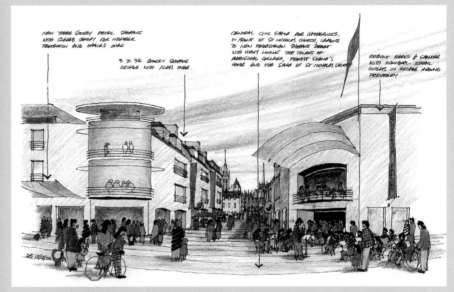

View from St Nicholas Street looking east along new pedestrian way linking Marischal College Provost Skene's house with St Nicholas Church – major intervention

Looking east along Broadgate – minimum intervention, retaining refurbished St Nicholas House

Axonometric views of the city centre help illustrate options for change, using simple colour coding to differentiate the proposals. A major exhibition in the city's art gallery took the strategy to the public and created a forum for events and debate.

A key issue in urban design graphics highlighted in this book is the choice between computer and hand drawings. In this case, a hybrid was selected: the strategy diagrams were produced using a computer, but the detailed drawings were hand-drawn, partly at the client's request because of the impression of inhabitation and liveability that can be achieved by expressive hand drawings.

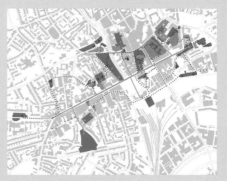

Strategy diagram incorporating interconnected urban squares and spaces

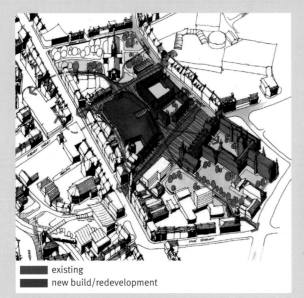

■ existing
■ new build/redevelopment

Higher intervention option incorporating redevelopment and environmental improvements

View into Robert Gordon University

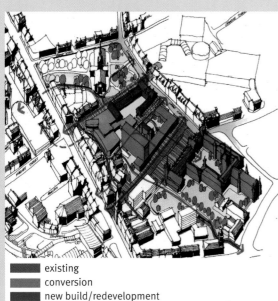

■ existing
■ conversion
■ new build/redevelopment

Low intervention option incorporating improvements to buildings, streets and public spaces

The green looking towards the refurbished Aberdeen Market

3.2
Base-maps

The majority of plans, diagrams and visualisations within this book would have been derived originally from a base map. It is common practice for base mapping to be derived from one of two sources:

- aerial photography
- Ordnance Survey©.

3.2.1 Creating base-maps from aerial photography

Photographic detail can distract the user from the message to be conveyed, and generally requires toning down to emphasise the overlaid information.

Reproduced courtesy of Cities Revealed

Step 1: Obtain/purchase photograph.

Step 2: Lighten the photograph or convert to greyscale.

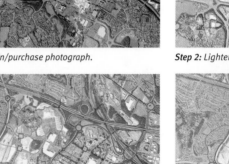

Step 3: Add illustrative information in a computer program making certain all relevant and important information is included and that colours are in sufficient contrast to distinguish features such as roads and buildings.

Step 4: Make overall final adjustments on colour balance and contrasts.

Watchpoints

- Most aerial photography is copyright and permission must be sought before reproducing it.

- Ensure the correct wording and copyright acknowledgement is clearly visible.

- Land and property boundaries may not be clear on aerial photographs and should be cross-referenced with Ordnance Survey© maps.

- Work out extent and coverage of photography required before purchasing.

- Ensure computer file formats are compatible before purchasing.

3.2.2 Ordnance Survey© base-maps

Ordnance Survey© maps are the most popular source for map bases, and are now available in a wide range of digital formats. In most cases the digital data requires editing before it can be used for illustrative purposes. Although the illustration style may look more like a diagram, the source data is reliable, measurable and to scale.

Watchpoints

- Ordnance Survey© material is copyright and permission must be sought before reproducing it.

- Any map or plan that has been derived from Ordnance Survey© is still subject to copyright.

- Ensure the correct wording and copyright acknowledgement is clearly visible.

- Work out coverage required before purchasing.

- Ensure computer file formats are compatible before purchasing.

- When editing, keep original files safe in case you need to refer back to them.

- Compare new base-map against original to ensure the clarity has improved.

Ordnance Survey Crown Copyright NC/A740836

Step 1: *Obtain/purchase survey map. Ensure that you obtain compatible file formats. The vector formats are generally supplied in either DXF, GML or NTF.*

Step 2: *Import map into vector illustration software. Surveyed maps are generally supplied in many layers and some layers may need switching off. Do not delete the layers as they may be required for reference later.*

Step 3: *Trace/redraw the relevant information you require. It is advisable to draw up a small area to develop a graphic style. Once you are satisfied continue this for the whole plan.*

Step 4: *Make certain all relevant and important information is included and that all colours have sufficient contrast to distinguish between different features such as roads and buildings.*

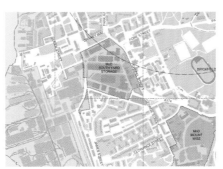
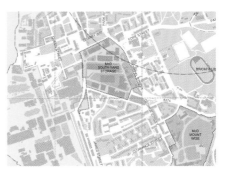

Step 5: *Add on illustrative information.*

Step 6: *Make overall final adjustments on colour balance and contrast.*

3.3
Using computers

Since the late 1980s, the use of computer technology in urban design has increased dramatically, but amid all the sophistication and quality of computer imagery, the essential message can be lost. We now have a more mature appreciation of the appropriate role the computer can play in expanding the graphical language of urban design. Modern computer software packages offer a powerful tool for creating images and drawings, but the range and sophistication of these packages can confuse the non-specialist.

3.3.1 Two-dimensional illustration

Illustrations (pictures or diagrams) make a subject easier to understand by sifting out unwanted or extraneous information to highlight what is important. Basic programs are available to create pictures and diagrams in vector form, when the accuracy of a comprehensive computer aided design (CAD) package would be unnecessarily complicated and require advanced skills. The line-based generation of images in vector form gives a cleanliness and sharpness to illustrations that can rarely be achieved by hand.

Primary role: Illustrating two-dimensional drawings, maps, plans and diagrams.

Characteristics: Generally produces crisp, sharp lines that can be softened by a variety of additional effects.

Level of accuracy: Can be scaled but not at high levels of detail.

Graphic capability: Excellent capabilities with numerous line types, colour fills, textures, patterns and effects to produce lively illustrations.

3.3.2 Computer aided design (CAD)

These packages are used to create very accurate scale drawings, and have transformed the technology of architectural design and construction. Their capability goes far beyond the range of images discussed in this book, but they can still be useful because they provide:

- the basis for 3-D modelling/ rendering and animation
- high levels of accuracy
- easy editing without having to redraw the whole image.

When a concept is to be translated into a masterplan, CAD makes it possible to resolve the plan to the level of accuracy required during subsequent detailing and implementation phases of the project.

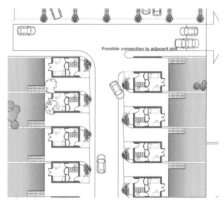

Primary role: To produce accurate working drawings in plan, section and elevation and form the basis of 3-D modelling.

Characteristics: Generally produces a hard-edged, finished look, although some versions have features such as 'sketch mode' to make the drawing look less definitive.

Level of accuracy: Very accurate and used for working drawings.

Graphic capability: Numerous line types, fills and patterns, but lacks special effects.

3.3.3 Geographical information systems (GIS)

These packages are used to access spatial data and present site-specific information via a map-base. The packages hold information in a database which is linked to geographical points, lines and areas. The database can hold information about social statistics, administrative boundaries, height, environmental designation etc.

They offer:

- excellent means of storing geographic information
- valuable tool for data presentation
- tool for interrogating multiple layers of spatial and tabular data
- tool for spatial analysis.

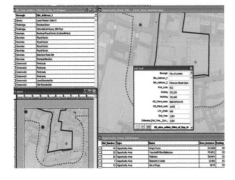

Primary role: To store, analyse, access and present spatial information with both geographical and tabular datasets.

Characteristics: Thematic maps presenting both quantitative data and spatial information. Information with a practical rather than graphically-distinctive look.

Level of accuracy: This can vary from highly accurate survey plans to less accurate thematic mapping, depending on level of detail and datasets used.

Graphical capability: GIS packages have increasingly sophisticated graphical presentation capabilities, but are not primarily intended for graphical presentation.

3.3.4 3-D modelling

These packages create virtual models using building blocks which include depth, allowing three-dimensional views to be generated.

They offer:

- powerful techniques to aid visualisation of buildings and places
- enhancement by rendering – adding realism
- rendering and lighting the model to vary mood and atmosphere
- photo-realistic renderings that are highly effective and user-friendly
- ability to explore and analyse options for massing or density
- solutions to three-dimensional design issues not otherwise evident.

Well-executed 3-D models are very persuasive and can easily be interpreted as finished or definitive designs. In the interests of credibility it is good practice to indicate the viewpoint, state the level of detail and define the purpose and status of the image. Whether at eye-level or from the air, viewpoints need to be fixed with care.

Primary role: To produce 3-D models to visualise a proposed development and to solve design problems such as massing, building heights and visual impact.

Characteristics: Produces very realistic virtual images.

Level of accuracy: Very accurate, although perspective, distortion and virtual views can be misleading and must be used correctly.

Graphic capability: Excellent graphic capabilities allow creation of virtually any surface, material or weather condition.

3.3.5 Animation

Once a 3-D model has been created with all its rendering and light settings, animation packages can be used to present the buildings and places as an animated sequence of views. The effect can be striking, particularly to people unfamiliar with the technique, but it can equally be seen as manipulative, and should be used with care and with a clear explanation of its purpose.

Animation offers:

- 'walk-throughs' or 'fly-throughs' that follow any selected path or route

- a potentially persuasive impression of how a place would actually work

- interactive modes with several viewing options

- a valuable tool for presentation and promotion

- effectiveness without full detail.

Animation is one of the most powerful techniques available. It is based on a sequence of static views.

Primary role: To walk/fly viewers through a development to give an appreciation of individual components, their interrelationships, massing and architectural style.

Characteristics: produces very realistic virtual places.

Level of accuracy: Very accurate but audiences have to rely on source drawings for accurate measurement.

Graphic capability: Excellent graphic capabilities can produce virtually any surface, material, weather conditions, shadows, time of day and night and different lighting conditions.

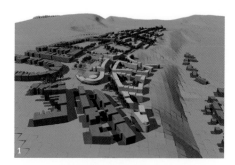

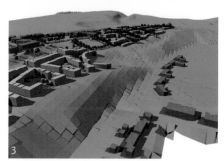

Series of animated high-level fly-throughs

Series of walk-throughs at eye-level

3.3.6 Photo/bitmap editing

This can be used to enhance 3-D images and photography, or for photomontage. Data is digital, and the software is particularly good for applying the colour and texture of materials. It is most useful for colouring and rendering images that have been created elsewhere or drawn by hand and scanned. It is not generally used to create accurate scale drawings.

Primary role: To edit and enhance bitmaps i.e. digital photography, scans, 3-D rendered models and to create photomontage and web graphics.

Characteristics: Very realistic and suitable for photography and 3-D imagery.

Level of accuracy: Not normally used for measurable work.

Graphic capability: With excellent graphic capabilities, bitmaps can be edited to any degree, even beyond recognition of the original image.

Original photograph

Enhanced photograph

Original 3-D model

Photomontaged landscape and background

Hand drawn artist's sketch

Final coloured sketch

Original photograph

Photomontaged 3-D model

Case Study 4

Newhall phase II, Essex

Client:
Newhall Projects Ltd

Consultants:
Roger Evans Associates Ltd

Challenge:
How can a graphics 'toolbox' assist the masterplanning of a new neighbourhood, relating movement structure, plot subdivision and building types?

Phase II of Newhall in Essex is a site planned to grow to a neighbourhood of 3,000 houses with a district centre and associated employment uses. The masterplan has been developed by the consultants as a continuous process, from establishing structuring principles and layout to detailed design codes for development parcels. The first step in the process was to produce, from a sketch plan of principal movement corridors, a layout that would set out:

- the street network
- development quantum and density
- basic landscape structure and urban form.

A graphics toolbox was devised which would establish a direct link between the spatial planning of the site and the consequences for street, plot and building design. The method has five stages.

Stage 1: Route hierarchy

The first stage was to devise a route hierarchy for the neighbourhood which established the patterns of movement. The hierarchy consisted of six route types which reflected the topography of the site; primary, secondary, tertiary, minor street, mews and footpaths.

Stage 2: Street sections

The next stage was to design cross-sections for each route on the plan; the first step toward transforming routes into streets. The sections define and articulate the kind of space that each route would become; their spatial qualities in terms of building frontage and threshold, width/height ratio, footpaths and cycleways, carriageways, planting, drainage, on-street parking and other features.

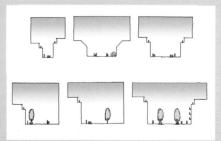

Street sections are designed for each movement route

Figure 1: Street sections
A sample of the street sections used in Stage 2. The sections:

- provide a direct link between the formal route hierarchy and the definition of the real dimensions and specifications that generate 'place'
- establish a third dimension to the design at an early stage in order to contribute toward continuing testing and review.

Stage 3: Building types

This stage identifies a range of building types along with design codes for their various relationships to the street and to individual plots. Plot series, setback, number of storeys, servicing, parking on the plot and private outdoor space were all addressed. Types ranged from four-storey townhouses and taller apartment blocks to detached villas and small row houses. These were matched with the street sections and route hierarchy to work up the next level of detail on the masterplan.

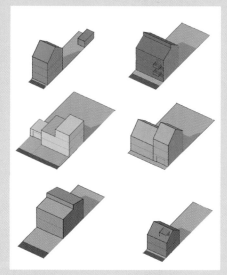

Figure 2: House types
A sample of the house types used that:

- indicates the level of necessary to specify only the relevant aspects for defining public spaces and private amenity space
- allow architectural freedom while ensuring the delivery of the public realm.

Stage 4: 1:500 scale modelling

This was created using the toolbox, which consisted of:

- the structure plan from Stage 1
- a set of street sections from Stage 2
- a palette of building types from Stage 3.

Using foam block models and a large base-plan, the composition of streets and spaces began, taking primary streets first and working down into smaller streets and the subdivision of development blocks.

Preparing 1:500 3-D model

Figure 3: Working up the masterplan with a 1:500 scale model

The process of master planning in Stage 4 using the set of tools developed in stages 1-3. The advantages of this technique are:

- using physical modelling allows a three-dimensional approach to placemaking and a continual testing and review of the emerging masterplan
- immediate review of development capacity, quantum and density throughout
- a set of tools developed from robust analysis of development form and capacity, providing a constant 'reality check'
- a large centrepiece model provided a focal point for lively and productive group design sessions and client reviews.

Stage 5: Orthogonal rectification

The model was photographed and orthogonally rectified (distortion and perspective corrected) so that it was true to scale in 2-D plan format. The masterplan was then transcribed, along with notation for the house types, storey heights etc, to enable a detailed analysis of development form and quantum.

Figure 4: Recording and orthogonal rectification of the model into two dimensions

A sample of the process involved in transcribing the masterplan into a form that is capable of detailed analysis in terms of development form and amount.

Working up the masterplan with a 1:500 scale model

Figure 5: 2-D rooftop masterplan.

Resultant masterplan

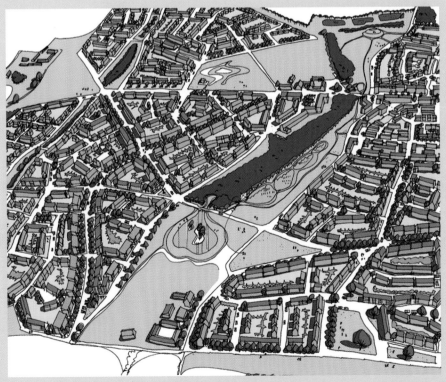

Aerial perspective of proposals

3.4
Synergy of styles

The most effective graphic presentations in urban design – reports, exhibitions or other promotional material – often include both hand-drawn and computer-generated images. Each has their rightful place in terms of the information and atmosphere they convey. They complement each other.

There are several ways in which both of these techniques can combine to produce a single image. For example, a computer-generated wire-frame model of proposals can be used as the base for a freehand perspective drawing which can then be rendered. Desktop CAD programs allow a wide range of viewpoints and angles to be tested as wire-frame bases before selecting preferred views.

The speed and flexibility of CAD modelling has made it simple to generate robust wire-frame underlays for any number of sketches or perspectives. Further information and detail are progressively added until the final drawing is vivid and animated, explaining the intended character of a place often more sympathetically than hard line computer-generated images can do. Using these techniques together can produce distinctive and unique images quickly and easily.

Step 1: Wire-frame model created of buildings in computer aided design program.

Step 2: Artist's sketch using the wire-frame model as an underlay to form the basis of the sketch.

Step 3: Sketch completed.

Step 4: Sketch scanned into the computer and coloured in photo editing program.

3.5
Desktop publishing (DTP)

Desktop publishing (DTP) combines all of the figures, diagrams, photographs, drawn images and visualisations produced as a single or a series of convenient documents.

Modern DTP programs give designers full control over document layout, typography and colour in a program that can be run on a basic computer. Documents can be printed using a laser printer or other print processes. It is also common to create portable document formats (PDFs) for printing, viewing on-screen or downloading from the internet.

The graphical quality of documents continues to rise as DTP packages become more sophisticated. They provide opportunities to brand and package projects for the client or the intended audience. This can be done by either creating standard templates in word-processing packages to customise the look and 'feel' of all documents, or producing bespoke designs in professional DTP software to give each project its own brand and identity. Whichever is preferred, graphic devices can help make documents eye-catching and easy and enjoyable to read.

An array of documents produced on desktop publishing programs

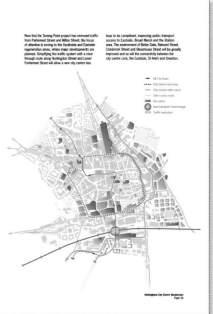

DTP spread combining text, photography and illustration

Watchpoints

- There is a limit to the graphical capability of word processing applications, although very basic DTP is possible.

- DTP requires training.

- Other software applications are normally used in conjunction with DTP – photo bitmap editing software to enhance imagery for example.

- Spell-check text at each stage of the DTP process.

- Start DTP when text and images are complete.

3.6
Software

Computer software offers a wide range of graphic presentation techniques to inform and communicate the urban design process. It is unlikely, however, that a single program will be sufficient for a complex project. Programs should be used only for the purpose for which they were designed, and by appropriately skilled users.

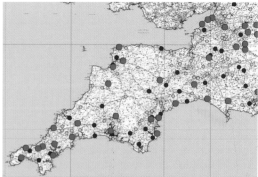
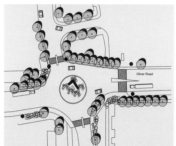
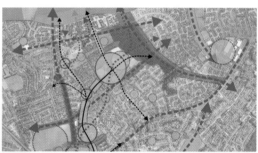

These images have been produced from a number of different software programs

Watchpoints

Computer software:

- Is designed specifically to undertake a primary role and should be used appropriately.

- Can easily and effectively add a distinct character, personality and style to the graphic output of a project.

- Packages have different levels of accuracy and should be used with this in mind.

- Some packages have limited graphic capability.

- One package will not normally produce the variety of illustrations required for urban design projects.

Graphical products in urban design

chapter 4

4.1 Reports and documents | 4.2 Exhibitions | 4.3 Leaflets |
4.4 Presentation drawings | 4.5 Posters | 4.6 Newsletters |
4.7 Digital presentations | 4.8 Websites | 4.9 Physical models

Urban design projects are presented
through a variety of products. The most
common fall within three main categories:

- print-based media
- screen-based media
- physical models

Each has a particular purpose in presenting
information to the intended audience.
This chapter shows examples of graphics
products and explains when and why they
are useful.

4.1
Reports and documents

Definition: Printed and bound documents containing detailed accounts of a subject through text, illustrations, photographs and tables.

Purpose: A convenient and accessible format for presenting and recording urban design project information. A series of reports may be produced, corresponding to project stages. Reports and documents may also become an archive of the planning and design stages of a project, used for future reference.

Production: Usually originated by desktop publishing (DTP) using computer programs to manage layout, text, images and colour. Printed by laser, digital or lithographic process.

Reports and documents:

- are available as standard templates in word processing packages or designed in DTP packages to brand project or by company/client
- are increasingly designed as loose-leaf format used, allowing easy updating over time
- full or selected report material may also be made available as CD ROM or on-line.

Watchpoints

- Diversity of graphic material (scale, detail, type of information, complexity) has to be managed carefully.

- Graphics must be clear and consistent.

- Page-by-page integration of text and graphics.

- Illustrations may be used for other products e.g. exhibitions, digital presentations. Origination should take versatility into account.

Example of good document design
Urban Design Compendium

Size: A4 portrait
Number of pages: 126
Print process: Lithographic

Front cover

Strong identity to front cover along with illustration of subject area

Contents

Clearly set out contents page with corresponding page numbers

Divider

Strong identity and consistent design to divider pages

Page layout

Page layout balances mix of text, illustrations, photographs and tables

Text hierarchy

Clear information to guide the reader around the document
- *document title*
- *page numbers*
- *headers/footers*
- *chapter title*
- *paragraph numbers*
- *headings/ sub headings.*

Back cover

Back cover design continued from front cover with all necessary contact information

4.1.1 Well designed and illustrated documents

*Local Development
Framework:
Plymouth City Council
(RTPI Award 2005)*

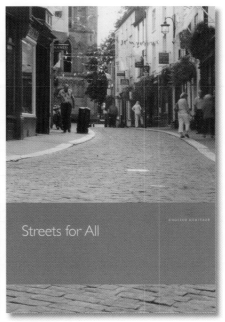

*Streetscape:
'Streets for All',
English Heritage series*

*Public Realm Strategy:
Towards a Fine City
for People –
Gehl Architects*

*Masterplan:
Nottingham City Centre 2005 – 2015
Nottingham City Council
in association with Urban Graphics*

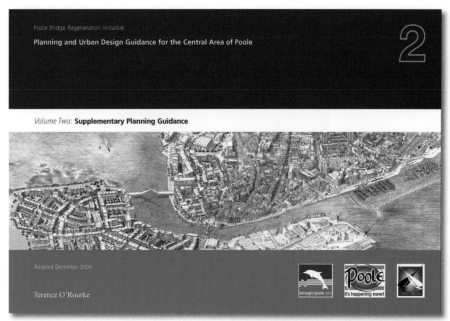

Poole Bridge Regeneration Initiative

Planning and Urban Design Guidance for the Central Area of Poole

2

Volume Two: **Supplementary Planning Guidance**

Adopted December 2004

Terence O'Rourke

Urban Design Strategy,
Poole Bridge
Regeneration:
Terence O'Rourke
& Partners

Lawley Design Codes:
English Partnerships

Upton Design Code:
English Partnerships

4.2
Exhibitions

Definition: Display of project material on panels or display units arranged as a sequence for viewing.

Purpose: Presenting information to the general public or to other audiences. Opportunity to make statements and engage individuals and groups with a single, accessible presentation.

Production: Range of portable panel units available (flat panel, pop-up, wire-framed structures or pull-up single canvas panels). Panels designed through desktop publishing programs printed direct onto large format panels. Artwork can be changed, panels re-used.

Exhibitions:

- if well-planned can bring a project to life
- can convey atmosphere and intention as well as information
- are more accessible to the general public than printed reports
- can display visual, aural and interactive techniques
- can provide valuable briefing for decision-makers.

Watchpoints

- Ensure the space is suitable (size/layout) for the information to be presented and the audience.
- Layout and sequence should suit the space as well as the information to be presented.
- Prior reconnaissance for measurements and photography essential.
- Critically review available information to sharpen and distil key messages.
- Strong graphic framework to unify material and guide audience.

Example of good exhibition design
Nottingham city centre masterplan

Venue: Council Ballroom, Nottingham
Turnaround time: Five days
System: Pop-up frame structure with magnetic tape to fix artwork panels
Stock: Heavy coated inkjet paper
Print process: Large format inkjet
Panel size: 2343mm x 781mm

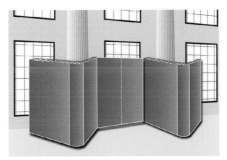

Early mock-up of exhibition to visualise three-dimensional space

Successful exhibitions inform the audience and encourage participation

Lighting brings out the exhibition even in the darkest of settings and arenas

Large, clear title to inform the audience immediately of the subject

Use mood images rather than descriptive text to portray the energy or atmosphere of a place

Captions or bullets are used to summarise text rather than long sentences or paragraphs (minimum font size for large panels is approximately 24pt)

Illustrations and photographs are enlarged for impact and ease of interpretation

All important information kept above at least 500mm from the ground

All electrics and cables are safely shrouded

Final exhibition

4.3
Leaflets

Definition: Single sheet or double-sided printed document folded to convenient size.

Purpose: Compact, user-friendly summary of key project themes/information, to support public consultation, exhibitions etc. and as project promotion.

Production: Using desktop publishing programs to combine text and images, large quantities can be produced at reasonable cost. An effective medium for communication.

Leaflets:

- are straightforward, flexible and are an effective medium
- convey core project message in a single document
- can be designed in a variety of formats
- creative graphics supported by wide choice of materials and techniques.

Watchpoints

- Concise and focused text.
- Images to be accurate and honest.
- Convey project quality and energy while providing information.
- Clear statement of project status and timetable – and what the audience can do.
- May be enlarged and used as posters.

Example of good leaflet design
Oxford, West End

Size: A4 Portrait when folded
Number of pages: 6
Print process: Lithographic

This well-illustrated leaflet not only informs local communities of project proposals but also encourages their involvement. This leaflet helped build community confidence and overall support.

Components:

- 6 page fold out spread
- summary text
- promotion of public consultation event
- project logo
- simple and contrasting colour scheme
- good balance of plans, photos and illustrations
- simple design aimed at a diverse audience
- attractive and user-friendly questionnaire
- freepost questionnaire reply form to collect local community views.

4.4
Presentation drawings

Definition: Two-dimensional presentation of an urban design project using scaled plans, elevations, sections and other views, generally printed on large standard format sheets (A2 – AO).

Production: Hand or computer drawn to scale. Can be rendered or colour enhanced.

Presentation drawings:

- can be used to present clear and unambiguous elements of project
- are a useful medium for discussion, review and negotiation
- can be valuable in presenting correct relationships between existing and proposed.

Watchpoints

- Presentation of detail may require large format drawings.
- Mounting and display height will affect ease of viewing when part of exhibition.
- Important to balance image against background white space.
- Mini-sets of reduced drawings useful for briefing and distribution.
- Normally presented as a series of drawings so keep keys, titles etc consistent.
- Mounting on boards will make them more durable.

Example of good presentation drawing
East Devon New Community

Size: A1 landscape
Print process: Large format printer
Stock: Heavy coated paper

Information included:

- project title
- drawing title
- originator
- title block
- scale bar/north point.

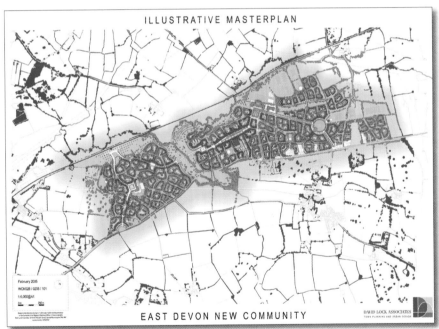

East Devon New Community Illustrative Masterplan

Presentation drawings are a very useful medium at meetings and workshops

4.5
Posters

Definition: Single sheet for public display.

Purpose: Advertise an event or promote proposals.

Production: Stand-alone page layout produced on desktop publishing programs and generally printed in large format.

Posters:

- can create instant attention
- provide an opportunity to present 'the vision'
- can be an overall energetic graphic.

Example of good poster design
Redhill Claypit

Size: A1 portrait
Print process: Large format printer
Stock: Heavy coated paper

This poster captures the immediate attention and interest of the audience with a minimum number of points, encouraging attendance to the event advertised to find out more.

This poster details:

- the project
- the area concerned and its context
- type of event
- the venue and times.

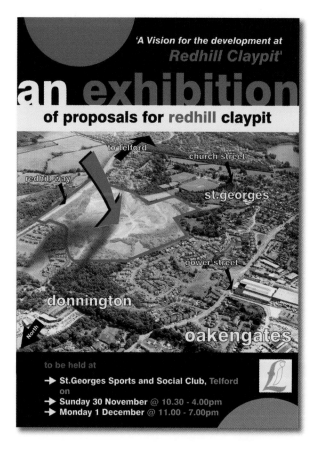

4.6
Newsletters

Definition: Regularly updated public information leaflets reporting progress on a project.

Purpose: Informing the community of the progress of the project, and encouraging continuing involvement. Newsletters may also include a questionnaire or other device for stimulating feedback.

Production: Desktop publishing programs to present project information in a consistent and repeatable format.

Newsletters:

- are a valuable, user-friendly medium for briefing and updating
- sustain interest and involvement
- are flexible enough to contain varied themes and topics
- present positive progress
- raise awareness.

Watchpoints

- Frequent use of familiar images, logos etc. builds recognition.
- Careful text/picture balance to reflect newspaper style.
- Co-ordinate with other project graphics.

Example of good newsletter design
Northstowe Update

An eye-catching document that uses the familiar newspaper layout combined with striking colour, distinctive graphics and pictures to attract attention. The professional production quality creates instant credibility, while images of places and issues familiar to local people stimulates interest. Text is easy to read and broken up into easily assimilated points.

4.7
Digital presentations

Definition: Visual/verbal presentation using laptop and digital projector.

Purpose: Presenting project overview or other information as briefing (public consultation, working session, invited group etc.)

Production: Prepared and edited on laptop or desktop computer using presentation software. A set of frames/slides can be printed out as an aide-memoire for the audience.

Digital presentations:

- are effective visual prompts for the speaker
- can communicate complex project information through accessible graphics
- can easily incorporate powerful and persuasive images
- can be made available as a CD (with voice-over) for personal use or to the public via a touchscreen facility
- can have themes presented either sequentially or as a build-up.

Watchpoints

- As few words as possible – concise and crisp text.
- Images and text reinforce and summarise what the presenter says – they are not a substitute.
- Consistent base for each image aids clarity and promotes a consistent message.
- Timed rehersal and editing essential.
- Needs as much preparation as any 'permanent' document.
- Use system fonts to avoid incompatibility.
- Check compatibility when transferred to another computer.

Example of well-designed slide
East Newport Sustainable Community

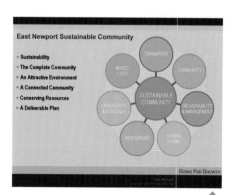

Example of poorly designed slide

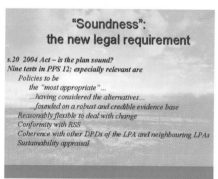

- simple graphics
- clear title
- concise text phrases
- bullets rather than long sentences
- single line of text to each bullet
- clean background
- contrasting colours
- legible typeface
- clear division of points
- minimum text size 14 point.

- too much text
- too many indents
- long sentences
- complicated background
- no contrasting colours
- over-use of italic type
- shadowed text
- no separation of points
- inconsistent text alignment.

4.8
Websites

Definition: Dedicated internet site set up by/on behalf of an individual, business, group or organisation.

Purpose: Providing readily accessible project information on demand at any time.

Production: Usually prepared by specialist website designer based on project information supplied.

Websites:

- are increasingly used to communicate and promote urban projects
- allow virtually unlimited concurrent access to shared project information
- can be easily updated as project develops
- are more flexible than print-based media
- can make a powerful and effective statement about the project.

Watchpoints

- Site should be structured to inform both general and specialist enquiries.
- As few words as possible – concise and crisp text.
- Should include a statement of current project status.
- Links for follow up/further information included.
- Sites need to comply with DDA guidelines (Disability Discrimination Act).

Example of a well designed website
www.dandad.org

- easy, consistent navigation
- minimum text
- use of menu pages to guide access to large amounts of information
- well composed and clear photographs/images
- sensible colour palette
- dark content text on white, printer-friendly background.

4.9
Physical models

Definition: Conventional physical display model, presenting site and built form in three dimensions, normally to a standard scale. Models vary in level of detail and realism.

Production: Many hand-made, but increasing use of computer-guided milling tools to create site contours and buildings. In-house sketch models often used to illustrate built form options. Fully finished models are usually produced by specialist workshops.

Physical models:

- are effective and accessible in presenting and marketing an urban project to a general audience
- clearly display contrasts of urban grain and building form, massing, landform and landscape
- present the broad structure of a place without being tied to detail
- can be viewed and photographed from all angles and viewpoints
- are readily viewed at all times without an electronic back-up
- cannot present the intended quality of a place or buildings at street level as effectively as computer-generated images or hand drawn views.

Watchpoints

- Full specification models can be costly, with lengthy lead times.
- Project proposals need to be 'confirmed' at an early stage.
- Can be difficult to update or modify if allowances for revisions/options are not made from the outset.
- Modelmakers require clear and prompt decisions from project team.
- Display, storage and transportation can be problematic.

Example of good physical model
Laganside masterplan

This model:

- clearly articulates the extent and layout of the development proposal in a contrasting colour and its integration with the surrounding context
- simply communicates the complexity of the infrastructure, road/rail bridges and river, their levels and their integration within the masterplan
- is a useful design tool which can be modified as the masterplan progresses
- articulates the built form and massing in relation to the scale of the site context, particularly the river, docks and bridges.

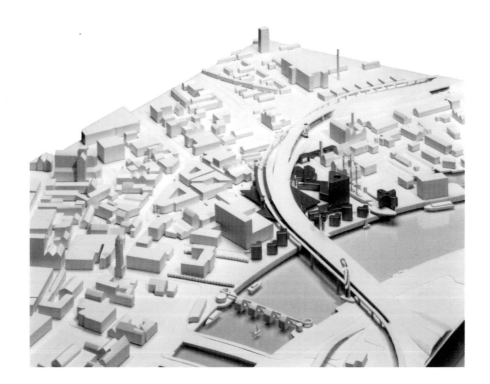

Managing graphics production

chapter 5

5.1 Briefing the designer | 5.2 Managing the output |
5.3 List of figures | 5.4 Project stages | 5.5 Print processes |
5.6 Printing in colour | 5.7 Budgets

There are several interrelated factors that will assist successful management of the graphics input to an urban design project.

In addition to the techniques explained in this book, and access to computer programs and other equipment, you will need:

- appropriate skills

- familiarity with the production process – from initial ideas to completed products

- access to appropriate printing capability and capacity

- a realistic budget for the products required.

5.1
Briefing the designer

It is the project manager's/director's responsibility to ensure that the core ideas and concepts created by the project team are accurately and effectively presented by the graphic designer. Getting the best graphics input to a project starts with appointing a graphics specialist with the right experience and the ability to work within a multi-disciplinary team. A clear project brief, setting out as far as possible what is expected and when, and the budget for each stage, will provide the basis for a good working relationship between the graphics specialists and the rest of the project team.

The expectations and requirements of the commissioning body or client also have to be taken into account. The project brief should have included any particular requirements for the graphics output. If possible, the graphic designer should be involved in agreeing the budget so that unrealistic expectations are not later disappointed, or found to have a detrimental impact on other parts of the project. Once the brief has been agreed it should be adhered to. Any necessary changes should be agreed and budgeted for as quickly as possible.

It is also important that the graphic designer is managed by one person, if not the project director, then a named individual. All members of the project team should work through that nominated person. Provided the designer has been given a clear brief as to what is required, the team should have confidence in the designer to produce output in an appropriate format and of an appropriate quality.

At the same time, urban design is a creative process and the final output is a consequence of the constructive relationship between all members of the project team. The essence of a successful project team is that all members are able to propose and challenge ideas. The graphic designer can help to sieve-out superfluous information and refine ideas to present them more clearly.

Watchpoints

Whether client or designer there are a number of points that jointly need to be resolved from the outset:

- Establish the brief and scope of work.

- Devise a method for producing the work.

- Define the outputs (i.e. list of products).

- Establish the program and deadlines for completion of key graphics products.

- Calculate and agree the budget (including a contingency).

- Ensure that any significant variations to the brief are costed and resources allocated.

5.2
Managing the output

This should be the responsibility of the graphic designer or a senior member of the graphics team, reporting to the project leader. All outputs should undergo a 'sign-off' procedure.

Watchpoints

- Agree what outputs are required at the outset and ensure the team have the required skills to deliver.

- Ensure you have all of the raw data available to complete the project – base-mapping, aerial photography etc.

- Agree within the team what techniques will best illustrate the messages (analytical, conceptual, measured or perceptual), but trust the judgement of the graphics specialists.

- Decide the method to be used for illustrations – hand drawn, computer generated or a combination of both.

- Decide the computer programs to be used by the team to ensure compatibility.

5.3
List of figures

One of the best ways of organising illustrations is by creating a list of figures that will be required, of which all team members are aware. This helps establish the schedule for creating the information for the figures and diagrams from the outset. A clear, logical numbering system should be created and digital files should be named to correspond. The graphics will come from a variety of sources and may be produced by different people. It therefore requires co-ordination. The example below indicates:

- the figure number
- the figure name
- the technique required
- who will produce the figure
- on which base-maps it should be overlaid (if applicable).

FIGURE NUMBER	FIGURE NAME	TECHNIQUE/METHOD	AUTHOR	BASE MAP
Figure 1	Context plan	Hand-drawn sketch	RK	1
Figure 2	Site plan	Measured computer illusration	BM	2
Figure 3	Overall masterplan	Hand-drawn masterplan on computer map base	NP	3
Figure 4	Development areas	Measured CAD plan	BM	3

A list of figures is an excellent way of organising the outputs and resourcing them

5.4
Project stages

The stages in graphics production reflect the refinement of ideas from initial concepts, through draft outputs to finished documents and presentations. These should be comfortably aligned with the stages of the project as a whole, but the project programme should incorporate the key stages in the graphics process.

Careful project preparation and close management will help ensure that project stages are being followed. Carrying out work in a sequence other than the logical stages of graphics production can be time-consuming and expensive; some graphics production is not easily reversible.

Although there may be several outputs to deliver – exhibitions, leaflets and so on, the core product is likely to be the main report from which most other products can be generated.

The programme opposite is based on a generic urban design project requiring the submission of a final report including text, data, illustrations, photographs, maps, etc.

Watchpoints

- Appoint a graphics specialist with the appropriate skills, experience and attitude.

- Establish the brief and scope of work and stick to it.

- Define the outputs (a list of products and figures).

- Calculate the programme.

- Allocate appropriate resources, for discrete components.

- Ensure that any deviations from the agreed brief are agreed by all parties and that any resources implications are acknowledged and accommodated.

Graphics production workflow programme

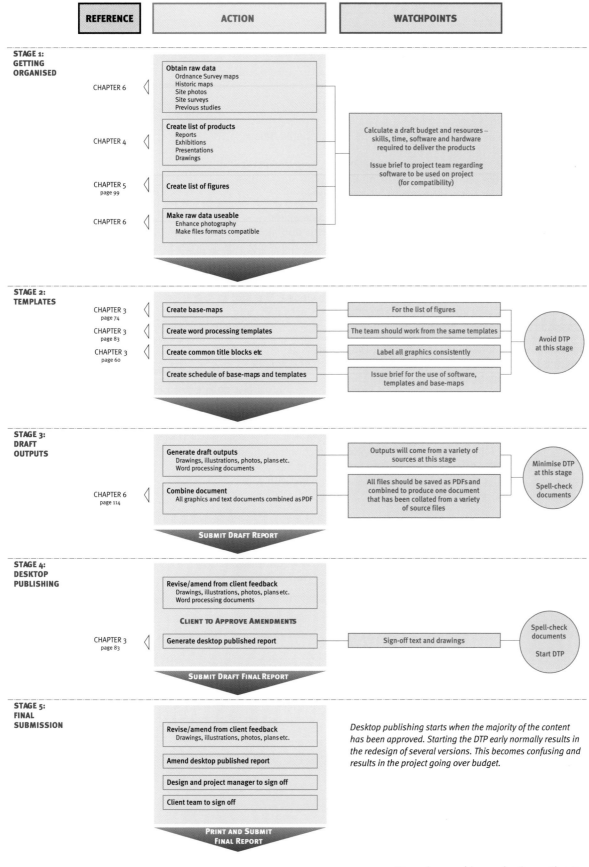

REFERENCE	ACTION	WATCHPOINTS

STAGE 1: GETTING ORGANISED

CHAPTER 6

Obtain raw data
Ordnance Survey maps
Historic maps
Site photos
Site surveys
Previous studies

CHAPTER 4

Create list of products
Reports
Exhibitions
Presentations
Drawings

Calculate a draft budget and resources –
skills, time, software and hardware
required to deliver the products

Issue brief to project team regarding
software to be used on project
(for compatibility)

CHAPTER 5
page 99

Create list of figures

CHAPTER 6

Make raw data useable
Enhance photography
Make files formats compatible

STAGE 2: TEMPLATES

CHAPTER 3
page 74

Create base-maps — For the list of figures

CHAPTER 3
page 83

Create word processing templates — The team should work from the same templates

CHAPTER 3
page 60

Create common title blocks etc — Label all graphics consistently

Create schedule of base-maps and templates — Issue brief for the use of software, templates and base-maps

Avoid DTP at this stage

STAGE 3: DRAFT OUTPUTS

Generate draft outputs
Drawings, illustrations, photos, plans etc.
Word processing documents

Outputs will come from a variety of
sources at this stage

CHAPTER 6
page 114

Combine document
All graphics and text documents combined as PDF

All files should be saved as PDFs and
combined to produce one document
that has been collated from a variety
of source files

Minimise DTP at this stage

Spell-check documents

SUBMIT DRAFT REPORT

STAGE 4: DESKTOP PUBLISHING

Revise/amend from client feedback
Drawings, illustrations, photos, plans etc.
Word processing documents

CLIENT TO APPROVE AMENDMENTS

CHAPTER 3
page 83

Generate desktop published report — Sign-off text and drawings

Spell-check documents

Start DTP

SUBMIT DRAFT FINAL REPORT

STAGE 5: FINAL SUBMISSION

Revise/amend from client feedback
Drawings, illustrations, photos, plans etc.

Amend desktop published report

Design and project manager to sign off

Client team to sign off

*Desktop publishing starts when the majority of the content
has been approved. Starting the DTP early normally results in
the redesign of several versions. This becomes confusing and
results in the project going over budget.*

PRINT AND SUBMIT FINAL REPORT

5.5
Print processes

There are many print processes available. Selecting the most appropriate largely depends on:

- budget available
- number of copies required
- physical size of media
- print quality.

The common print processes employed in home, office or bureau are listed below:

- **Inkjet printing** is mainly aimed at the home user. It is relatively cheap to set up although costly to maintain. The print quality and resolution can be outstanding. A4 and A3 are the common print sizes although A2 is also available.

- **Laser printing** is best suited to offices as printers are larger, and designed for multiple users via a computer network. Their main advantage is double sided printing (in some cases) and the number of A4/A3 copies they can output quickly.

- **Digital printing** is carried out within a bureau. The machines used are generally too large to sit within offices and require specialist operator knowledge. The print quality and resolution is very good. Printing larger than A3 is easy and can be finished in various ways (coating, binding etc).

- **Lithographic printing** is also undertaken by a bureau. The quality is generally excellent but because of the high set up costs, it is best suited to documents that are required in large quantities.

- **Inkjet large format** can be carried out by both offices and bureaus. They are best suited for large format such as posters, presentation drawings and exhibition materials.

Printing in colour is more complex than modern computer printing technology might suggest. With the number of print processes available and the choice of file types to print from, there are many variables that need to be considered. Working with your printer should help you overcome any difficulties.

PROCESS	QUANTITY	TURNAROUND	QUALITY	SIZE	UNIT COST
Inkjet	1–25	Minutes	Very good	A4–A3+	High
Laser	1–50	Minutes	Very good	A4–A3+	Medium
Digital	1–500	1-2 days	Very good	A4–A3+	Medium
Litho	500+	5 days	Excellent	A4–B1 roll	Low
Inkjet large format	1–25	Minutes	Very good	A2–A0 roll	High

The table above is a general guide for the commonly used print processes

5.6
Printing in colour

Printing in colour is more complex than modern computer printing technology might suggest. Not only is there a considerable amount of preplanning required but also digital computer files need to be set up correctly to ensure a quality output. Most computer programs will have default print settings. These will need resetting according to the print process (print shops and bureaus will normally advise).

Sensible print planning will normally lead to more economical ways of printing. All involved in the print process should allow enough time for print planning/management and proofing to ensure that they meet the specified deadlines.

Watchpoints

Consideration of the following points affects both cost and turnaround time:

- Page size.

- Number of pages.

- Type of stock and its weight – certain stock is more suited to certain print processes (printers will advise).

- Quantity of print run.

- Quality of print.

- Binding/finishing methods.

- In-house or external printing – external printers have to co-ordinate your requirements with other commitments.

5.7
Budgets

Project briefs should describe or specify what outputs are required during the course of and at the end of a project. This should include the content, format and quantity of reports or other material corresponding to pre-agreed stages. Such information allows these outputs to be costed with a fair degree of accuracy, but it is easy to overlook additional costs, such as those associated with printing reports, preparing exhibitions or duplicating CD ROMS. If these outputs are not defined fully – or at all – in the project brief, then they will have to be agreed before the project progresses to subsequent stages.

The graphic designer should be involved from the outset in costing the project brief. To produce a realistic project budget calls for knowledge of how to deliver the outputs to the quality required using the production method appropriate within a given cost. An experienced designer can foresee potential problems which might affect the budget, quality of output or delivery dates. This can avoid the dilemma of having consumed the graphics budget before the end of the project and still having to produce the outputs required by the brief.

All print and production processes have their own particular turnaround times. In addition, depending on which production process is chosen, the computer files may have to be reformatted. While computer technology can be a great time-saver in any form of production, careful preplanning is essential to ensure that it is correctly applied to produce the graphic outputs, whether screen or print-based.

Watchpoints

- What are the outputs and have they been costed?

- Have the graphics inputs been properly resourced and costed?

- Remember – graphics can take longer than you expect!

Images and Information

chapter **6**

6.1
Aerial photography

There are three main types of aerial photography used for urban design project.

Vertical photographs are taken immediately above the subject area from an aircraft using a special camera used for mapping and survey purposes. Taken at low altitude using high resolution film, they can capture great detail of planting, buildings and surfaces. It is usually possible to scale from the photographs.

Vertical aerial photography – Courtesy of Cities Revealed©

Oblique photographs are taken at a distance from the subject area to provide an overall visual impression of an area. They are usually flown specifically for the project, to provide the information and background needed to produce a composite image of the site, including proposals. Unlike vertical photographs, they provide an indication of topography and the relative height of buildings. They are more difficult to scale from due to perspective.

Oblique aerial photography – Courtesy of Airphoto©

Terrain photography is vertical photography draped over a terrain map to provide a 3-D visualisation. This is particularly useful when establishing the contoured land-form from the air or a desired view from the ground.

Terrain photography courtesy of Get Mapping©

Most aerial photography achieves very high levels of accuracy – distortion and other errors can be corrected by specialist software, making it possible for these images to match the accuracy of Ordnance Survey© and other survey maps. In general aerial photography provides the following benefits:

- An accurate visual record of what is on the ground
- An accurate visual record of landscape and environment in different seasons or weather conditions
- Vertical photography can be Ordnance Survey© accurate
- Can be cheaper than maps (although not a substitute).

Watchpoints

- All photography is copyright and should not be reproduced without the consent of the owner. Copies or reproductions are normally subject to a copyright fee that is preset by the owner.

- Check file formats before ordering.

- Check file sizes as they can be very large and unmanageable by slower computers.

6.2
Site photography

Building up a comprehensive visual record of the characteristics of a site and its setting with photographs taken from key viewpoints can help when analysing, designing or promoting it. Having a stock of high-quality images of a site always justifies the effort involved in taking them.

Whether using film or digital technology to photograph a site, the same principles apply. Successful site photography depends upon following a few basic rules to ensure usable and informative images.

Rule of thirds – a time honoured device used by artists and designers, long predating photography.

The rule of thirds
Imaginary lines drawn to divide the image into thirds both horizontally and vertically help to compose an image in a way that feels instinctively attractive and arresting. Locating key elements along one or more of the imaginary lines will draw the eye immediately to them.

Time of day
Depending on the time of day and season, a site may be heavily shadowed or subject to failing daylight by mid-afternoon. Either could lead to unfavourable or inadequate images, while sunlight and clear conditions are likely to produce a positive result.

Zoom lenses
In the case of a digital zoom, the magnification of pixels can, depending on the resolution of the camera, cause a loss of detail and sharpness in the image.

Optical lenses re-create the image by magnifying it. With an optical zoom, the focal length of the lens is physically changed, comparable to walking closer or further away from the subject. There is no loss of image detail apart from when a wide angle zoom is used. Very long focal length zooms will tend to flatten the image, with loss of perspective.

Original photograph

Photograph using digital zoom

Original photograph

Photograph using optical zoom

Weather conditions

Poor lighting conditions can make images flat and lifeless. Taken on bright, sunny days, colour photographs are more vibrant and seem to have greater three-dimensional depth. Conversely, the high contrast and shadows of bright weather can conceal useful and important detail that is evident in overcast but clear weather. Bad weather can create a negative impression of a place, but striking images of weather systems can add drama to images. Choose the weather conditions that suit the purpose of the images.

Viewpoint

A more successful composition in a photograph may achieved by changing the viewpoint. Apart from moving it to right or left, a higher or lower camera position can produce a more interesting image or reveal a new perspective on a familiar subject.

Overcast weather can make images look flat and lifeless

Brighter weather brings life to the image

Different viewpoints of the same location can drastically alter the composition

Viewpoints plan

In presenting a set of site photographs, it is essential that the locations from which they were taken and the direction of view are clearly indicated on a plan. These are commonly shown by an open V with a number or letter reference. The reference plan should include enough information to place the views in context.

Panoramas

It may be impossible to capture the full breadth of views of or from a site, even with a wide angle lens, which will in any case distort the view visible to the eye. Standing further back is one solution, but this may be ruled out by obstructions or the land-form. Another option is to overlap several photographs taken from a single point.

With a digital camera, these shots can be 'stitched' together using software programs to produce a panorama. Such programs are sometimes supplied with the camera. For best results a tripod is advisable as the level of the camera should remain constant. Pictures should be taken with some overlap based on a common feature at the edge of both adjoining frames. It also advisable to take panoramas from different locations to build up a comprehensive impression of the site.

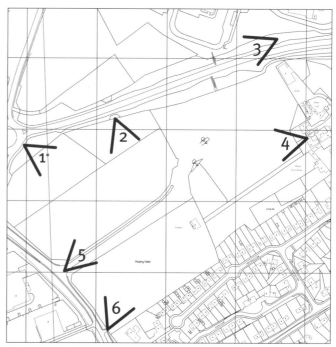

Photographic viewpoints plan

Panoramic photography used to capture the entire width of a site

6.3
Setting out to photograph

Success in site photography is down to more than point-and-shoot. It needs preplanning as well as a degree of luck on the day. An eye for detail and local distinctiveness can help the project team build a library of representative images of a site and its setting, such as public art, building details, local activities and people. These can breathe life into reports and convey the character of a place more effectively than words.

Watchpoints

- Pack spare batteries, memory sticks, films for the non-digital, lenses – even a spare camera.

- A site plan which has been marked up to identify key viewpoints and areas to be recorded, so that nothing of importance is missed.

- An APS format camera (non-digital) can prove useful on its 'panorama' setting to record a wider view without the need to stitch pictures together.

On-site watchpoints

- Views from a high vantage point can reveal the overall structure of the site.

- It is worth taking a series of sequential views of an urban site, so that these can later form the basis for a before-and-after sequence of views to illustrate design proposals.

6.4
Enhancing photography

Photographs taken on site or from a general library may turn out not to be entirely satisfactory for project or presentation use. In such cases, photo retouching and enhancing can be employed. These can often achieve dramatic improvements in image quality.

Photo enhancing and retouching
This is a process in which a digital image made from a scan or digital photograph is altered to meet an acceptable standard. This means generally correcting image flaws such as poor contrast, colour or sharpness. The process can also be used to change the mode or format of an image to suit different applications.

While there is no substitute for a well-taken photograph or flawless scan in the first place, problems are sometimes unavoidable. In these cases a photo-editing software package can be used to correct flaws, and provide the opportunity to enhance elements of the image or correct its size and resolution to provide the required output.

Once an image has been digitised it can be enhanced in many different ways. Common photo-enhancing methods include:

Cropping
To make the images look stronger as a composition and to concentrate on the area required, the image can be cropped using the selection tool. The image can also be rotated before cropping to adjust its vertical alignment.

Brightness and contrast
Adjusting brightness and contrast makes the light areas lighter and the dark areas darker. This can often help an image that looks 'flat' by bringing certain elements forward and others back. There is some danger of losing detail in the image if this technique is taken too far.

Hue and saturation
Adjusting the hue and saturation of the colour in an image can allow the colours to be made to look richer and more vibrant. It does this by identifying the dominate colour for an area of pixels and adding more of that colour. The colour balance can also be changed, allowing images which may have yellowed or browned through age to be restored.

Sharpness
Although the focus of an image that is already taken cannot be adjusted, it can be sharpened by using the sharpen filter. This works by decreasing the amount of colour detail in the image and, flattening some of the colours, making the image look sharper, but the capability of this facility is limited.

Correcting over and under-exposed photographs
Over- and under-exposed photographs are the result of either too much or too little light entering the lens. This can be corrected in some cases by adjusting the brightness and contrast, but the image can often emerge looking pixelated or grainy. Highlights, midtones and shadows need to be adjusted independently of each other by using the 'levels' control. This allows shadows to be made lighter while leaving the highlights or vice versa.

Watchpoints

- Enhancing and editing can only improve the image to a certain degree.

- Always compare the original image to the enhancement.

- Over-enhanced photographs can look artificial.

6.5
Ordnance Survey©

It is impossible to imagine planning without the information base provided by Ordnance Survey© in the United Kingdom. It holds accurate and detailed mapping information for the whole of Great Britain and can supply this in both digital and paper copy.

For day-to-day project use in urban design, there are a wide range of formats and products available from Ordnance Survey©, including:

- **OS MasterMap®** Database and on-line service with highly detailed and flexible digital maps. Data is held in themed layers to allow users to pick and mix type and extent of information needed.

- **Land-Line®** Very detailed digital maps showing individual building footprints and the layout of roads, surveyed at scales down to 1:1250.

- **Superplan®** Site-centred highly-detailed maps as paper print-out or CD ROM, via e-mail or on-line.

- **Landplan®** 1:10000 scale coloured map which simplifies more detailed map data and which can be printed out on demand, site-centred if required. This series is also the basis of a new generation of 1:10000 scale raster (bitmap) maps.

- **Land-Form PROFILE®** and **Land-Form PANORAMA®** Landscape contour information which can be used to produce 3-D computer images.

Ordnance Survey© has scanned historical maps from the 19th century onwards. These can be overlaid with modern maps to identify changes in the landscape and development over time. It also has raster data which can provide 'backdrop' computer-based maps at various scales. These can be viewed on-screen allowing a user's own information to be electronically overlaid.

All Ordnance Survey© material is copyright and subject to licensing agreements for each of its products. It is normal practice to obtain a licence number from Ordnance Survey© along with the correct notation for reproducing their maps.

For further information visit: **www.ordnancesurvey.co.uk**

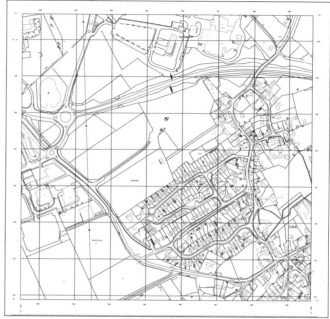

Land-Line extraxt reproduced by kind permission of Ordnance Survey© Crown Copyright NC/A740836.

Watchpoints

- Ordnance Survey© is available in print and digital formats.

- Specify the appropriate file type (DXF, NTF, PDF or bitmap) when ordering.

- Ordnance Survey© digital (vector only) is made up of several layers that separate all boundaries and features. With OS Mastermap you can select the layers you require.

6.6
Types of image

Whether a 3-D model or a 2-D illustration, static images can be divided into two categories – raster or vector. Each has unique qualities that are exploited differently, and can be combined.

Raster/bitmaps images

Raster (also known as bitmap) images include digital photographs, scans or images created with a photo-editing software programs. Such images consist of a grid of colours comprised of pixels. Each pixel is assigned a colour value and a location on the grid. Bitmap images are resolution-dependent. This means detail or definition can be lost if they are re-scaled on screen, or printed at a lower resolution than that for which they were created.

There are generally two applications for raster images – screen or print – and they must be used appropriately. For screen images such as websites and digital presentations RGB images (Red, Green, Blue – the primary colours of light) are used. For print-based images CMYK (Cyan, Magenta, Yellow – the primary solid colours – and Black) are used. As each pixel contains a lot of information, bitmaps generally produce large file sizes. Some bitmap types use compression to reduce file sizes. When sharing bitmap files it is important to know which applications support the file type.

Vector images

Vector images or objects are made up of mathematically-defined lines and curves called vectors, which describe an image according to its geometry. Vector objects are resolution-independent. They can be scaled to any size and printed at any resolution without losing detail or clarity. Popular commercial CAD and graphics programs create vector graphics. Attributes of these lines/curves can be adjusted in weight (thickness) and colour, along with the colour within an enclosed object. With these variables it is possible to specify or design custom-made illustrations to suit any purpose.

It is common practice to embed both raster and vector graphics in one file for a variety of uses. The most commonly used file format is known as PDF.

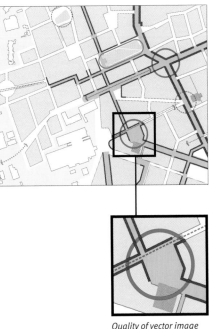

Quality of vector image retains clarity when magnified

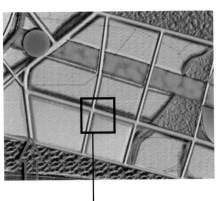

Quality of raster image becomes pixelated when magnified

6.7
Portable document format (PDF)

Portable Document Format is an electronic file format created by Adobe™, initially to provide a standard form for storing and editing publishable documents. Documents in PDF format can be viewed easily and printed by users via a variety of computer programs. They are the most popular document-sharing file format and are very popular on the world-wide web.

PDFs are generally a second-generation file format; the files are initially created in other software programs and then re-created as PDFs. Vector, raster and typefaces (fonts) are contained within the PDF. When creating PDF files the user has considerable control over the following characteristics:

- **Pages:** It is possible to select which pages are required as PDFs, particularly useful when working with large files consisting of several pages. Rather than processing the whole document, it only processes the pages required, saving time.

- **Bitmaps:** It is possible to sample the resolution of a bitmap at the scale required. This is particularly useful when reducing the file size by reducing resolution. The file size can be reduced still further by selecting the appropriate compression for the bitmaps such as JPEG or LZW.

- **Fonts:** When working with fonts it is essential that the fonts used are embedded or converted to curves/paths. If the font used is not embedded, it is possible that the PDF will substitute a multiple master font that provides the best match. If fonts are saved as curves they will no longer be a font but a curve, which makes them practically uneditable.

- **Colour modes:** It is possible to set the colour mode to suit the final purpose of the PDF. This can assist in reducing the file size and helps print bureaus, as the majority will work in CMYK mode. When printing in colour with digital or lithographic output always use the CMYK mode. When viewing on screen use the RGB mode. When the final output does not require colour but tints of black (greys), use the greyscale mode.

- **Pre-press:** It is common practice to send PDF files to printers for digital and lithographic print runs. When publishing PDFs the document can be set with crop and registration marks to assist in the finishing process. With the increased adoption of PDF, an industry standard has been defined – called PDF/X – to ensure more reliable pre-press data interchange. This file format standard is now widely used by designers to create a file that they can be confident will be printed predictably and correctly by the service provider, whether it is a commercial print job printed on one site, or an advertisement placed in many publications and printed across the world. Printers and publishers should ideally be provided with digital page layouts that can be confidently run through pre-press without requiring reworking or causing errors, ensuring they meet customer expectations of the final product.

6.8
Paper sizes

	mm
A0	841 x 1189
A1	594 x 841
A2	420 x 594
A3	297 x 420
A4	210 x 297
A5	148 x 210

An enlargement from a paper size to the one above i.e. A4 to A3 is always 141%
A reduction from paper size to the one below i.e. A0 to A1 is always 71%

A0 to		A2 to		A4 to	
	A1 = 71%		A0 = 200%		A0 = 400%
	A2 = 50%		A1 = 141%		A1 = 283%
	A3 = 35%		A3 = 71%		A2 = 200%
	A4 = 25%		A4 = 50%		A3 = 141%
	A5 = 18%		A5 = 35%		A5 = 71%

A1 to		A3 to		A5 to	
	A0 = 141%		A0 = 283%		A0 = 568%
	A2 = 71%		A1 = 200%		A1 = 400%
	A3 = 50%		A2 = 141%		A2 = 283%
	A4 = 35%		A4 = 71%		A3 = 200%
	A5 = 25%		A5 = 50%		A4 = 141%

6.9
Scale conversions

1:50 to		1:1000 to		1:10000 to	
	1:100 = 50%		1: 500 = 200%		1:2500 = 400%
	1:200 = 25%		1:1250 = 80%		1:5000 = 200%
	1:500 = 10%		1:2500 = 40%		1:25000 = 40%
			1:5000 = 20%		1:50000 = 20%

1:100 to		1:1250 to		1:25000 to	
	1:50 = 200%		1:500 = 250%		1:10000 = 250%
	1:200 = 50%		1:1000 = 125%		1:50000 = 200%
	1:500 = 25%		1:2500 = 50%		
	1:1000 = 10%		1:5000 = 25%	1:50000 to	1:10000 = 500%
					1:25000 = 200%

1:200 to		1:2500 to	
	1:50 = 400%		1:1000 = 250%
	1:100 = 200%		1:1250 = 200%
	1:500 = 40%		1:5000 = 50%
	1:1000 = 20%		1:10000 = 25%
	1:1250 = 16%		

1:500 to		1:5000 to	
	1:100 = 500%		1:1000 = 500%
	1:1000 = 50%		1:1250 = 400%
	1:1250 = 40%		1:2500 = 200%
	1:2500 = 20%		1:10000 = 50%
			1:25000 = 20%

Illustration and photography credits

We thank the originators for permission to reproduce artwork and photography. We have tried to contact and credit the copyright owners of all images used in this book. Illustration and photography is credited on each page from top to bottom, left to right. The authors will be happy to receive requests for any credits missed, and these will be incorporated in future editions.

We would also like to thank the landowners and agents whose foresight in appointing teams that recognise the importance of graphic communication in the urban design process has helped enrich this book.

Further reading

Basic Cartography	R. W Anson and F. J Ormeling	*International Cartographic Association and Elsevier Science Limited 1995*
Book Design	Andrew Haslam	*HNA Books 2006*
Cartographic Design and Production	John S. Keates	*Longman Scientific & Technical 1989*
Creating Excellent Buildings	CABE	*CABE 2003*
Creating Successful Masterplans	CABE	*CABE 2004*
Creating Successful Neighbourhoods	CABE	*CABE 2005*
Envisioning Information	Edward R. Tufte	*Graphics Press LLC 1990*
How Maps Work	The Guilford Press	*The Guilford Press 1995*
Information Graphics	Robert L. Harris	*Oxford University Press 1999*
Introductory Cartography	John Campbell	*Wm C. Brown 1991*
Look at this	Adrian Shaughnessy	*Laurence King Publishing 2006*
Manual of Typography	Ruari Mclean	*Thames & Hudson Ltd 1980*
Responsive Environments: A manual for designers	Bentley et al	*Butterworth 1985*
The Urban Design Compendium	English Partnerships	*English Partnerships 2000*
The Concise Townscape	Gordon Cullen	*The Architectural Press 1996*
The Dictionary of Urbanism	Robert Cowan	*Street Wise Press 2005*
The Image of the City	Kevin Lynch	*The MIT Press 1960*
The Urban Design Handbook	Urban Design Associates	*W. W. Norton 2003*
Towards an Urban Renaissance	Urban Task Force	*Spons Press 1999*
Urban Design Guidance	Urban Design Group	*Thomas Telford Publishing 2002*
Urban Villages and the making of communities	The Prince's Foundation	*Spons Press 2003*

Useful websites

www.architecture.com
www.cabe.org.uk
www.cabespace.org.uk
www.cartography.org.uk
www.dandad.org
www.landscapeinstitute.org
www.ordnancesurvey.co.uk
www.rudi.net
www.rtpi.org.uk
www.tcpa.org.uk
www.the-aop.org
www.udal.org.uk
www.udg.org.uk
www.urban-graphics.co.uk

Graphic design by **Urban Graphics**:
Bally Meeda
Jon Knox
Rakesh Kumar
Rob Smith

w: www.urban-graphics.co.uk